Seeing Our Faith

Janet Hodgson has worked and written extensively in the area of mission. She developed the *Healthy Churches* resources with Robert Warren for Church House Publishing and before retirement worked as a missioner in the Diocese of Durham. She has a PhD from the University of Cape Town, and she taught in the Department of Religious Studies for 15 years.

She is the author of *The Faith We See* (Inspire) and *Making the Sign of the Cross* (Canterbury Press) and lives in South Africa.

Seeing Our Faith

*Creative ideas for working with
images of Christ*

Janet Hodgson

CANTERBURY
PRESS
Norwich

© Janet Hodgson 2011

First published in 2011 by Canterbury Press
Editorial office
13–17 Long Lane,
London, EC1A 9PN, UK

Canterbury Press is an imprint of Hymns Ancient and Modern Ltd (a
registered charity)
13a Hellesdon Park Road, Norwich, Norfolk, NR6 5DR

www.scm-canterburypress.co.uk

British Library Cataloguing in Publication data

A catalogue record for this book is available
from the British Library

Scripture quotations are from the New Revised Standard Version of
the Bible (Anglicized edition), copyright 1989, 1995 by the Division of
Christian Education of the National Council of the Churches of Christ in
the United States of America. Used by permission. All rights reserved

978 1 84825 061 1

Typeset by Regent Typesetting, London
Printed and bound by
CPI Antony Rowe, Chippenham

CONTENTS

For Jay

Family, and friends in McGregor

FOREWORD

Seeing Our Faith is a remarkable resource for a wide range of discipleship groups, for church councils and for those preparing for confirmation. The focus on the world Church and the diverse contextual approaches to the Person of Christ draw all of us into a deeper empathy and insight. We are guided away from our missionary-age presumptions about broadcasting the blond Jesus and welcomed inside the indigenous images of Christ where people have kept their own names for God. This book helps us to live in vivid context St Paul's words that in Christ all barriers between human beings are broken down and go on being subverted by the response of people to the Christ who is always moving towards them.

This book brings together an extraordinary range of resources. I can assure readers are coherent and useful precisely because they have been tested in Janet Hodgson's own practice as a leader of workshops with a wide range of communities and groups. When Janet and I were colleagues in the Diocese of Durham, she led a series of workshops with me and members of the parochial church council of the parish where I was the incumbent. I was deeply moved and challenged personally by working with a variety of images. More importantly, I witnessed not only other lives being changed profoundly before my eyes but also positive developments in the dynamic of the PCC as a group.

One of the challenges which Janet brought to us was to our assumptions about our native spirituality. We had assumed that while we might refer condescendingly to the spirituality of Native Americans in Canada with whom Janet had worked in the past; we were affronted by the very idea that there might be a discernable spirituality of the North East of England which drew on a particular history and industrial landscape. Of course, it was obvious and liberating when we faced it. That was the point: we were brought face to face with a means by which we might properly appropriate the real story of Jesus and our heart-and-mind pictures of him at work in our lives, not as a dead person in the past to revere, but as our living friend and Saviour whom we could picture in our midst.

Janet makes the clear distinction in the book between images of Christ and the nature of icons as themselves sacraments of the Incarnation. The distinction is a proper one but it does not diminish the impact of the images as invitations into a more incarnated experience of Christ. The images can be three-dimensional with clips of film and sculpture, as well as the engagement with pictures and posters. For those of us who deal most naturally in pictures, the workshops free us to look upon the Word and no longer feel guilty about how we relate to Christ in prayer and imagination. For those of us who are mainly word smiths, the workshops are a gentle introduction to how we might integrate our reading of the words of Scripture with eloquent images in a way which avoids all idolatry.

Icons are often seen as anchors of the divine in our midst. The images available here are at the least windows which might lead us into new landscapes of the Spirit. The material here to assist meditation and prayer is first rate. There is something very special about keeping silence together as a group, knowing that each individual is responding to God uniquely but held in a shared turning positively to Christ.

This turning to Christ is what the book is all about. Janet's whole ministry has been to be a catalyst in the releasing of Christians to be partners in the mission of Christ where God has placed them. The workshops and all the associated materials are made available not primarily for self-improvement but so that as larger groups or as twos and threes we can participate more richly in the building of the kingdom. Because this is the kingdom of our Lord Jesus Christ, it draws in the nations, favours the poor and the outcast and brings peace and righteousness together. Janet uses a prayer of her fellow South African, Desmond Tutu which I commend with this whole book:

> Goodness is stronger than evil;
> Love is stronger than hate;
> Light is stronger than darkness;
> Life is stronger than death;
> Victory is ours through Him who loved us.

+Stephen Conway
Ely
March 2011

PREFACE

This book is about working with images of Christ as a way of enabling people to explore, nurture, share and celebrate their faith through a wide variety of means. It can easily be used by lay people for lay people, while at the same time providing hard-pressed clergy and church workers with a wealth of accessible resources to enhance their ministry.

Although some of the material has been drawn from a previous publication, *The Faith We See: Working with Images of Christ* (Peterborough: Inspire, 2006), it has been completely revised and reworked. Much new material has been added, including guidelines on collecting images, and numerous illustrations, together with programmes for workshops, talks, stories, Bible studies, discussion starters, exercises, meditation and prayer, and liturgies, all using imagery. Most of this material, including images of Christ from around the world, can be downloaded from a companion CD-ROM, making it a very user-friendly workbook.

As with its companion piece on crosses – *Making the Sign of the Cross: A Creative Resource for Seasonal Worship, Retreats and Quiet Days* (Norwich: Canterbury Press, 2010) – this book has been designed to reach a broad range of people of all ages, be they churchgoers, seekers, non-churchgoers or people of other faiths. It demonstrates the myriad ways in which images of Christ may be used, whether for personal faith formation or group awareness; for teaching or preaching; in evangelism and mission; for theological reflection and Bible study; in preparation for baptism and confirmation; in private devotions and corporate worship; or as aids in prayer and meditation. All the material has been tried and tested over many years. Although most of my work has been in Anglican settings (embracing the whole range of church traditions), it is thoroughly ecumenical and has been used successfully in multicultural situations in England, Canada and South Africa.

A pick-and-mix approach has been adopted so that the material can be used in programmes of varying lengths and with any size of group. For those who would like to delve into deeper theological aspects, there is enough food for thought and exploration. But one of the main aims of the workbook is to motivate lay people to explore the mystery of the Incarnation without making things too complicated.

Above all, a special effort has gone into making the workbook fun to use as well as enlightening.

I came from a teaching background in Religious Studies in the University of Cape Town, and with my postgraduate studies involving extensive fieldwork, I moved to the United Kingdom in 1987 to work for the Church of England. For a year and a half I was the first Visiting Fellow at the College of the Ascension in Selly Oak, Birmingham. The college was run by the United Society for the Propagation of the Gospel (USPG: Anglicans in World Mission), an Anglican mission society which celebrated its tercentenary in 2001. This was an invaluable opportunity to broaden my knowledge of how Christ has been incarnated in different cultures and contexts in other parts of the world.

1 – The Presentation in the Temple
(Luke 2.25–38)

During my time as Mission Adviser for USPG in the Dioceses of Oxford and St Albans, I built up my collection of images of Christ until they numbered around 5,000, encompassing both historic European examples and contemporary ones from around the globe. After I moved to Durham Diocese in 1994 as Adviser in Local Mission, this resource continued to be used countrywide until I returned to South Africa in 2001. It was precisely because working with images proved so effective that I have tried to set down as much as I can of my experience. My hope is that others will be inspired to use the material in this workbook to enrich their faith and that of others, as it has enriched mine.

I would like to express my sincere gratitude to all those friends who have supported me in this work over the years, added to my collection of images, hosted me and held workshops in various venues, survived my enthusiasms, and guided me through my personal pilgrimage of faith.

In England, I am deeply indebted to a number of faithful friends – Stephen Conway, Bishop of Ely but former Archdeacon of Durham; the Revd Canon Alison White, and the Revd Geoff and Monica Lowson in Newcastle Diocese; the Revd

Jeremy Dussek in Birmingham; the Revd Fr Tim Pike, CMP, in North London; the Revd Robert Cooper in Thorpe Thewles; the Revd Sheila Day in Billingham, and the Revds Mary and Paul Judson in Hartlepool, Durham Diocese.

In South Africa, my family have continued to give me unfailing support, only too happy that I am kept busy and fulfilled. In McGregor, the small village where I live, I am endlessly grateful for a loving and caring community who know me as 'Janet, the book' (as distinct from 'Janet, the cook' – not my forte). In particular, I would like to mention Corrie van der Colff, my Pilates trainer who has kept watch over my well-being; Francois Holmes, who lights candles and offers many prayers on my behalf; my sister, Gillian Lord; Bridget Rose, who supplies me with nourishing treats; Yvonne Courtin, who backs up my drafts; Christine Lawley, for printing cards of some illustrations; Geoff and Heather Neil, who work wonders with images on the computer; and Ann Snaddon, whose creative genius has provided a wealth of illustrations.

It has been a joy to work once more with Dr Natalie Watson, Senior Commissioning Editor for SCM Press. I would also like to thank Rebecca Goldsmith for her meticulous handling of the text, and Leigh Hurlock who has once again created such an imaginative cover.

Finally, I am deeply grateful for the friendship and wisdom of the Revd Jay S. Kothare, a retired Anglican priest in Manchester. He has been a tireless reader of my drafts, and throughout the process of writing this book has been endlessly helpful with research, suggestions, theological insights and original contributions. His support through all the vicissitudes of writing has been a source of unlimited inspiration and enlightenment.

Acknowledgements for permission to publish their material must be given to the following:

The Rt Revd Stephen Conway for being bullied into doing the Foreword.
Angela Ashwin, for the use of prayers in the leaflet accompanying the wooden Holding Crosses.
Archbishop Desmond Tutu, for the use of his prayer.
The Revd Donna Bomberry, Co-ordinator of the Anglican Council of Indigenous People, for use of the logo for the former Council on Native Affairs, Canada, 1980s.
The Revd Robert Cooper, whose photographs are a continual inspiration.
The late Revd Richard Shorten, for use of the African Madonna and Child image from the church at Wembezi, Natal, South Africa.
Catherine Wakeling, archivist from USPG: Anglicans in World Mission, for the use of my Native American and African Liturgies, published in *Transmission* in 1993, and illustrations from various SPG publications.

Ann Lewin, for permission to print her poem, 'Impaled', and for information about the Carne cross.

The Revd Canon Alison White, Newcastle, Anne Bedford and Jane Banks, the Revd Jeremy Dussek, Vicar of Moseley (St Mary and St Anne), Birmingham, and Billy Kennedy of Temenos, McGregor, for imaginative feedback on working with images; and also Jeremy's help with some reflections and selection of colour pictures for the CD-ROM.

Dr Esther de Waal, for permission to use a Celtic prayer.

Rose de la Hunt, for her image of 'The Master'.

Ann Snaddon, for 43 ink and wash illustrations.

Janet Marshall and Canon Morriat Gabula for their contributions.

We gratefully acknowledge the use of copyright items. Every effort has been made to trace copyright owners, but where we have been unsuccessful we would welcome information that would enable us to make appropriate acknowledgements in future reprints.

ILLUSTRATIONS

GUIDELINES FOR USING THE BOOK

2 – Latin American Madonna and Child

Pick-and-Mix Planning of Programmes

The contents of the chapters have been set out in detail so as to allow for a pick-and-mix approach in planning how best to work with images of Christ in different situations. Programmes have been designed to give some structure to a range of options, depending on the nature of the event. The selection of relevant material would be determined by the purpose of the exercise, the number of people involved, their background and age, and the time available.

Each programme contains a wide selection of material to suit every need. This might be for an hour, an evening, half a day, a full day, a weekend, part of an extended course, a quiet day or a few days on retreat. The content could include talks with background information, hands-on work with images and the sharing of responses, topics for discussion including Bible studies, thought-provoking material for reflection, or guidance on praying and meditating with images. The workshops vary in length so that extra modules can be added as required. Guidelines are given regarding timing, but this again is flexible. Worship material using visual aids is provided throughout, as are plentiful handouts and illustrations.

Some of the images incorporated in the workbook or on the CD-ROM relate specifically to the text, while others can be used in meditation, prayer and worship. All are designed to show how artists from different parts of the world, both past and present, have portrayed Christ in every imaginable way and in every possible medium. This could be in terms of their indigenous culture and ethos, in symbol or in abstract art, as an expression of their faith in their everyday lives, or in situations fraught with trauma and suffering. No matter what, the immediacy of the imagery allows us to enter into the artist's experience and make it our own. 'Seeing our faith' through the eyes of others can have a lasting impact, as is abundantly clear from the many stories we have gathered from a cross-section of people in quite different contexts.

Practical Arrangements

Practical arrangements need to be dealt with at the start of every programme, however long it may last and whatever the purpose. These include:

- Welcome, and introduction to the purpose of the programme.
- Inviting people to introduce themselves by name and, if appropriate, where they have come from and why (curiosity, new learning experience, pressurized by minister or friend, etc.).
- Available facilities and space, inside and out – for worship, talks, workshops, quiet times, meals, relaxation.
- Worship arrangements.
- Timing of breaks for tea or coffee and meals (a shared meal may be appropriate, or on a quiet day or retreat some people may prefer to bring their own refreshments).
- Toilet facilities.
- Any times of silence, and whether this includes meals.
- List of times when the facilitator will be available, if required, for private discussion or hearing confession (if ordained).
- Allowing time to answer questions, both at the start and at the end.

Resources Needed

- Name tags if required.
- Comfortable seating in a pleasantly heated environment (neither too hot nor too cold).
- Sufficient handouts for programmes, worship, talks and stories.
- Images of Christ – most workshops would require an adequate selection, from postcards to A4 posters (can also be in books).
- Long (coffee) tables on which images can be displayed around the room. Screens or pews are useable but not so effective.
- Equipment to project images from CD-ROM either onto a blank wall or screen.
- Bibles, printed liturgies, prayer manuals, hymn and song books with music, large sheets of paper and felt-tip pens, writing material – where needed.

3 – El Greco Christ

- CD player if music is to be used during worship, with extension lead, and suitable music.
- Symbols and aids to be used in worship as indicated – images of Christ, holding crosses, prayer beads, incense, candles and matches.
- Workshop material as indicated.
- Refreshments as required.
- All the necessary utensils and sacramental elements if the Eucharist is to be celebrated, or food and drink for an *agapé* meal.

The purchase of this book entitles you to photocopy or print out handouts and worship material for personal or non-profit use as required for information, workshops, worship and meditation.

Handout 1
Collecting Images of Christ

A collection of images can easily be assembled by tapping into a variety of sources. The image can vary in size from small prayer cards and postcards to A4 posters. Pictures of Christ, and Christlike figures, can be cut out of mission society magazines and newspapers, or photocopied if permission has been given. The *Church Times*, for example, regularly prints religious pictures from recent publications together with art in contemporary exhibitions and interesting new acquisitions in local churches. These include crosses and crucifixes, sculptures, Stations of the Cross, paintings, stained-glass windows, tapestries and other devotional imagery. This material should be mounted on a firm backing (old files, cardboard, etc.), so as to survive rough handling, and it can also be laminated.

The *Daily Telegraph* published an excellent six-part series, *AD: 2000 Years of Christianity*, to mark the Millennium (now in book form), while *Anglican World*, the quarterly journal of the Anglican Consultative Council, reproduces unusual religious art and artefacts from different parts of the Communion. Quality reproductions of religious artwork can also be found in inexpensive and readily available publications featuring classical European artists like El Greco, Rembrandt and Michelangelo.

Books can be borrowed from libraries from both the art and religious sections. Children's books often have original illustrations too. The internet has provided a new source of images obtainable through search engines. Selected sites are given at the end of the book, some offering a couple of hundred images, although the quality may vary. British church buildings have preserved a historic selection of sacred art and, where permitted, photos can be taken. Art exhibitions in religious venues or galleries sometimes provide illustrated catalogues (see 'Further Resources').

Museums, art galleries, specialist art shops, and church and cathedral bookshops are the best source of postcards and posters, as are places of pilgrimage like Walsingham, Iona and Holy Island, Lindisfarne. Christmas and Easter cards are another readily available source, as are calendars and prayer cards. The mere fact of asking people to be on the lookout for suitable images as they travel at home and abroad is enough to awaken interest, whether this is for a personal collection or a combined effort. Any faith community can soon gather enough material for a workshop; and adding to the collection is half the fun. Visits to a Catholic country provide the richest pickings in churches, museums, art galleries and religious bookshops. Works of art from past centuries need to be balanced with a selection from different cultures and contemporary Western images.

The Benedictine nuns of Turvey Abbey in Essex have produced a brightly coloured collection of laminated sets of posters and illustrated booklets with meditations in their *Jesus, Our Life* series – *Jesus, Our Light*; *Jesus, Our Way*; *Jesus, Our Hope*; and *The Footsteps of Jesus* – as well as a set of Stations of the Cross.

From a multicultural perspective, Lat Blaylock has published two packs of images under the title *Picturing Jesus: Worldwide Contemporary Artists* (Pack A, 2001 and Pack B, 2004). Each pack contains 16 A4 picture cards, telling the story of Jesus from the cradle to the cross, and beyond. The artists represent a host of different countries in five continents as reflected in their rich variety of style and content. Although this material has been designed as an educational tool, and the creative teaching and learning approaches are aimed at different Religious Education levels, it has a much wider appeal. The reverse side of each image contains an outline sketch of the picture, a Bible text, the appropriate narrative story and discussion material. A 24-page guide provides further information, together with a range of imaginative exercises.

Margaret Cooling's work, *Jesus Through Art*, is another creative resource for teaching RE though art which would be suitable for any age group seeking to learn more about their faith. Large colour prints, spiral-bound for whole-group use, are combined with extensive notes and teaching material. At the moment, Cooling's publications are out of print but could be obtained from a library or religious resource centre.

Probably the most widely used resource in the last few years is the *Christ We Share* pack jointly produced by USPG: Anglicans in World Mission, USPG Church of Ireland, Church Mission Society and the Methodist Church (1999, 2nd edition, 2000). Described as 'a world church resource for local mission', it includes 32 A5 cards with 12 full-colour acetates for overhead projection, two booklets with theological information and explanatory notes on the images, activity sheets, ideas

for worship and a resource list. This has been followed by a similar but smaller pack, *Born Among Us*, with images of the nativity from around the world. Both packs have been used in schools and further education establishments, as well as in church groups of every description.

In the 1930s and 1940s, SPG as it then was published three booklets of paintings by Chinese and Indian artists and a few African sculptures to depict the life of Christ. Most of the Chinese pictures came from Roman Catholic churches. They are particularly interesting as an early example of inculturation in which the gospel is expressed in terms of Chinese culture using typical Chinese artwork. Similarly, Alfred Thomas, the Indian artist, has portrayed Jesus and his disciples in Indian settings and has drawn

4 – The Shepherd and His Lamb

on Indian symbolism to express his Christian faith (see various illustrations).

In an African milieu, a set of more than 60 *Vie de Jesus Mafa* paintings (1973) provides a colourful depiction of the Gospel story among the Mafa people in northern Cameroon. The difference is that they are the work of an unknown French artist rather than an indigenous interpretation of Christianity. Commissioned to illustrate the Gospel readings from the Annunciation to Pentecost, the artist got local villagers to enact a series of biblical scenes and then painted the resulting tableaux. The setting is African, as is the symbolism, but some feel that the inherited Christianity of the colonists is still pervasive. Images from the set are widely available as postcards and posters, and are popular in workshops.

Over the years, Christian Aid and CAFOD (Catholic Agency for Overseas Development) have produced challenging seasonal resources with a justice and humanitarian focus, together with worship material from different countries. CAFOD's distribution of the Miserior hangings and other material from Aachen in Germany are particularly effective. See, for example, the Lenten Veil, *Hope for the Marginalised*, and the Haitian and Ethiopian hangings. Taizé in France offers a selection of uncluttered images on postcards and posters with an ecumenical dimension. These go well with their many CDs and tapes of religious chants.

Duplicates are always useful, especially with popular images such as Holman Hunt's *The Light of the World*, Albrecht Dürer's *Praying Hands*, Salvador Dali's *Crucifixion* and *Christ of St John of the Cross*, and Margaret Tarrant's very English Christ in *Loving Shepherd and Lesser Brethren*. Artistic merit is never an issue in the exercises, nor are any contentious elements. The very nature of trying to 'see our faith' through imagery is enough of a challenge.

5 – Bread and Wine

Symbolic imagery of Christ is a genre in itself. The earliest symbols include an anchor, the mast of a ship, a fish (*ichthus* in Greek), and the signs for *alpha* and *omega* (the beginning and the end). Crosses and crucifixes are the most prolific symbols, providing a never-ending complexity of shape, size, form and decoration. Other symbols commonly found in church buildings, illuminated manuscripts, religious artefacts and stationery include Christ the light, Lamb of God, Trinity, bread and wine, corn and grapes, chalice, crown of thorns, halo, pelican, peacock, palm leaf, circle, triangle, and many more. All are relevant in a collection of images, and many people prefer to work with these rather than a human depiction of Christ. The difficulty is in trying to interpret significant symbols from other cultures.

Nearly 4,000 images from my collection have been deposited in the education department of the Shrine of Our Lady at Walsingham, Norfolk. But even with a modest collection it is possible to put together a set of images around a particular theme. This can be used for teaching, group work or meditation. The focus may be cultural – Native American, Filipino, British, African or Indian. Or it may be historical, with images relating to the Coptic, early Christian, Celtic or Renaissance periods. Or it may feature the work of one artist (like Stanley Spencer or the sculptor Peter Eugene Ball), a group of artists (like the Pre-Raphaelites or contemporary English painters), or artists from a particular country. In a church context it is particularly helpful to group images around Gospel themes (Christ calling or sending out his disciples, healing and teaching, Mary and Martha, Peter's denial of Christ) or the main liturgical events in the year (like Passion Week and Easter).

Prayer of Hildegard of Bingen (*c.* 1098–1179)

Be not lax in celebrating.
Be not lazy in the festive service of God.
Be ablaze with enthusiasm.
Let us be an alive, burning offering
before the altar of God.

1

WHY IMAGES OF CHRIST?

6 – Christ, the Master

Seeing Our Faith

One of the defining marks of our contemporary culture, which has profound implications for how we present the gospel, is that we now live in an audio-visual age. We are constantly bombarded by competing images, and the world around us reverberates with a cacophony of sound. From advertising, the internet, mobile phones, television or shopping malls, 'the medium is the message'. In this postmodern context, feeling is likely to take precedence over thought, the subjective over the objective. For the Western Church, this means that the post-Reformation and post-Enlightenment religion of the word is hopelessly 'out of sync' with the audio-visual reality of our daily lives. No wonder that a Church which relies on a cerebral expression of the gospel finds itself increasingly irrelevant and redundant.

People who are seeking a living faith are more likely to respond to a presentation which incorporates the intuitional, emotional, relational and numinous aspects of life, rather than the propositional and rational alone, if at all. In our mission to reach people where they are, we should concentrate less on verbalizing our Christian beliefs and focus more on how we can experience and communicate with them through imagery, symbol, music, song, story, dance and drama.

In working with images of Christ, we use as wide a selection of pictures and symbolic representations of Christ's life, teaching and ministry as possible. This would include copies of paintings and sculptures in every possible medium; and of stained glass, calligraphy, frescoes, mosaics, crosses and crucifixes, manuscript illustrations, woodcuts, tapestries, posters, prayer cards, internet images, symbols, word pictures, biblical texts, and the like. Some portrayals of Christ span centuries of religious art across Europe, with Coptic images from Ethiopia providing a more exotic touch. The majority, however, are modern, and encompass a global Christianity, contemporary Western imagery being as compelling as that from Asia, Africa and Latin America. The images have been conceived in every imaginable context and every possible cultural setting, ranging from the lifelike to the abstract and symbolic.

Together, the images represent the incarnate God in a rich diversity of moods and modes, challenging us to see Christ afresh, whether we are churchgoers or not. For those accustomed to wrestling with questions of faith at a cerebral level, the visual impact of the images opens up a new world of experience, which can reach into the very depth of our being. This is all about 'seeing with the eyes of the heart': an exploration that engages one's most intimate feelings and brings one closer to God. At the same time, the images encompass both the particularity and universality of the life of Christ, offering surprising new insights.

The assumption is often made that images work best in a non-book culture. Indeed, they can be of great value in freeing people up from any inhibitions. No special requirements or qualifications are needed. All start in the same place, laity and clergy alike. However, working with images may be even more beneficial

7 – The Wedding Feast at Cana

in a highly cerebral culture where the left side of the brain is dominant: where rationality and logic take precedence over feeling and emotion, analytical thinking over intuition and imagination, where people have become alienated from their symbolic inner worlds.

Images of Jesus are visual iconic representations of the Incarnation, endowed with colour, shape, contour and movement, and embedded in the gospel narratives. By disengaging Christ from his own specific historical and geographical context, they allow people to meet him in their very own situation, whatever that may be and whoever they are. At the same time, one has to be aware that there are those for whom Scripture is the only revelation, the only medium of communication of the mystery of Christ. The incarnate word and the written word are seen as correlated. We need to ask, therefore, why working with images is such an important way of helping us to 'see our faith'.

Handout 2
Programme for a One-off Event, Half a Day, or Part of a Course, with a Celtic Prayer

Refreshments are provided as required.

Why Images of Christ?

	Celtic Prayer or Denominational Worship
5 minutes:	Welcome and any notices. The leader and participants introduce themselves.
10 minutes:	Introductory Talk: 'Seeing our Faith'.
1 hour:	*Handout 3: Talk: 'Why Use Images of Christ?'*
	Topics for discussion.
	Bible study 1: 1 John 1.1–3.
15 minutes:	Break.
15 minutes:	*Handout 4: Talk: 'Images and Icons'.*
	Handout 5: exercises – 'Seeing Our Faith'.
30 minutes:	Exercise 1: 'Images of Christ in your Church'.
30 minutes:	Exercise 2: 'Biblical Titles for Jesus'.
30 minutes:	Exercise 3: 'Using Christmas and Easter Cards as Images of Christ'.
5 minutes:	St Richard's Prayer.

Celtic Prayer

Bless to us, O God,
The sun (or moon) that is above us,
The earth that is beneath us,
The friends who are around us,
Your image deep within us,
The day (or rest) which is before us. Amen.

Handout 3
Why Use Images of Christ?

Some people have misgivings about working with images of Christ, citing injunctions from the Old Testament (OT) against 'graven images' (Exodus 20.4–5, Deuteronomy 4.12–18). Admittedly, the OT does refer to Yahweh as manifesting himself indirectly through wind, fire or a still, small voice; or, at best, through revelations to his anointed prophets. In those days, any likeness of Yahweh was regarded as nothing short of blasphemy.

However, traditional accounts support the view that the early Church departed from the OT prohibition against using sacred images in Temple worship. Evangelist Luke himself was credited with having 'written' an icon of the Virgin with the Christ Child. Significantly, icons were said to have been written down as though they were revelations from God and not painted like a work of art. Thus, the Christian Church, in spite of its Jewish origins, encouraged the belief that sacred images were not mere artistic decorations but genuine instances of divine revelation. Similar records include the many versions of the Veil of Veronica depicting an imprint of Christ's wounded face on his way to Calvary, and busts of Jesus in various catacombs and Roman mosaics. The Shroud of Turin is one of the best known examples of a supposed image of Jesus in liturgical usage.

The Iconoclast or image-breaking movement emerged within the Eastern Church as a direct consequence of the impact of Islam, which rigorously subscribed to the Old Testament ban on sacred images. We are indebted to Saint John of Damascus (670–749) for leading the struggle to win back the recognition of sacred images as a valid component in Christian liturgy. Saint John, citing Philippians 2.6–7, argued: 'When he who is bodiless and without form empties himself and takes the form of a servant, and is found in a body of flesh, then you draw his image.'

Depicting the invisible God is, indeed, wrong, but, in the Incarnation where 'the Word became flesh' (John 1.14), the invisible Yahweh of the Old Testament becomes visible as part of his new dispensation for the salvation of his entire creation. This then makes it permissible to depict Jesus Christ, the second person of the Trinity, in human and earthly terms. As a matter of fact, it is vital for a believer to be able to see Jesus if they are to see God. As Jesus declares: 'Whoever believes in me believes not in me but in him who sent me. And whoever sees me sees him who sent me' (John 12.44–5). The very tactile nature of this encounter with Jesus is reflected in the opening phrases of 1 John: 'We declare to you what was from the beginning, what we have heard, what we have seen with our eyes, what we have looked at and touched with our hands.'

In his famous work 'On The Divine Images', John of Damascus has this encouraging message to the future makers and users of divine images, including us:

> Depict Christ's wonderful humility, his birth from the Virgin, his baptism in the Jordan, his transfiguration on Mount Tabor, his sufferings which have freed us from our sufferings, his death, his miracles which are signs of his divine nature made manifest in human flesh. Show his saving cross, the tomb, the resurrection, the ascension into heaven. Use every kind of drawing, word and colour![1]

We end with the words of Pope Gregory VII (died 1085), which he addressed to an image-bashing bishop: 'We venerate icons and images but we do not adore them. We adore, however, only God the invisible Father, his visible Son Jesus Christ our Lord and the Holy Spirit, which is the source of all life, visible and invisible.'

Topics for discussion

- From early on, our churches have had sacred images displayed in many different forms. Discuss the role they have played over the centuries in the teaching, preaching and liturgical ministry of the Church.
- Share your thoughts about a particular image in a church that has left a lasting impression on you and strengthened your faith.

Bible study: 1 John 1.1–3

Read the text slowly and out loud.

The one significant distinction between the OT prophecy and the good news of the NT is that Yahweh, whom nobody, not even Moses, had been privileged to see, has now become manifest in Jesus for everyone to see. Though, unlike John, we do not encounter Jesus in the flesh, yet we witness him in images.

- The same image turns into an idol when we begin to adore the image. Discuss the meaning of this giving possible examples.
- Have images helped or hindered you in your personal worship? How?

Handout 4
Images and Icons

A proper distinction must be made between images of Christ as we use them in workshops, and icons as venerated in the Orthodox Church. For Orthodox believers, the Christian image is thought to be an extension of the Incarnation. Icons are thus seen to possess an inherent sacred quality. Since the first century they have been used in worship and as a means of instruction. In earlier times, the majority of people were illiterate and relied on wall paintings in their churches to learn about their faith. Vestiges of this tradition remain in ancient cathedrals and churches throughout Europe and Britain. The 'Doom' was a popular theme, as was the crucifixion, flanked by the Ten Commandments.

8 – A Byzantine icon

Icons are not illustrative art. Rather, the symbolic language of their imagery corresponds with the contents of Scripture, as do the liturgical texts.[2] In an Orthodox church, word and image carry equal weight in the preaching of the gospel, evident in the central position of the iconostasis, the screen dividing the nave from the sanctuary. As sacred images, icons are believed to mediate between the sacred and the profane worlds. Viewing an icon is viewing

God himself. Touching an icon is touching God. Only a trained *staretz* or spiritual leader has the authority to conduct such an exercise.

As sacred art, the painting of an icon, on enamel, metal, mosaic or wooden panels, is rigorously controlled by tradition. The iconographer should lead a holy life, while the sacred canon dictates faithfulness to historical themes, and to certain rules of composition and technique. This includes the preparation of materials and colours; geometry and perspective; gesture, clothing and facial features of the subject; and symbolic stylization.[3] Any deviation is thought to diminish the religious content of the icon. Its beauty is not as an object, but in the divine likeness which it represents. Its role is not to bring us closer to the natural world, but rather to allow us to enter into the sacred realm, inviting us 'into the stillness of contemplating heavenly realities'.[4]

Images of Christ are not objects of adoration. We see them as secular religious art: simple, down-to-earth pictorial representations of Christ without any pretensions to an innate, divine or mystical aura. Whereas icons are a medium to the divine; and while one meditates on an icon, one meditates with and through an image. Through the images we are confronted with Christ, who is always with us, sharing in our journey and inviting us to explore new ways of being his disciples.

As a tool for 'doing' theology together, the images provide a means to reflect on our faith in the Incarnation through art instead of through the written or spoken word. In Western practice, we are used to consulting reference books and relying on scholarly expertise. In other parts of the world, a populist oral theology is normative, being expressed through extempore prayer, praise, preaching and witnessing. What the images offer is an innovative third alternative in 'doing' theology, giving people the unfettered luxury of space to try and fathom what the Christian faith means to them. At the same time, their faith is enhanced as they encounter Christ in other cultures and contexts.

Because working with images usually involves a group, relationships are integral to the experience. Moreover, the communal context is at the heart of how we relate to Christ and how he relates to us. By using images to express our corporate life in Christ, we begin to experience the pulsating dynamic of a community of faith under the lordship of the living God.

9 – Stained-glass Christ, All Saints' Church, Robertson, South Africa

Handout 5
Exercises: 'Seeing Our Faith' and St Richard's Prayer

What we tend to take for granted are the many images of Christ which surround us in church, as well as those we exchange as Christmas and Easter cards. Biblical titles for Christ are yet another form of imagery. The following exercises are designed to show us how we already see our faith, often without realizing it.

Exercise 1: Images of Christ in Your Church

- Working in pairs, go round your church building and list all the images of Christ you can find – on altars, statues, pulpits and lecterns, crosses and crucifixes, stained-glass windows, paintings, banners, biblical texts, Sunday school drawings, altar frontals, kneelers, etc. Make as long a list as you can.
- After a set time bring the group together to share their lists and reflect on how Jesus is visibly present in the church.
- Discuss: What impact might these images have on worshippers?
    What impact might they have on visitors?
- Do we need a study guide to inform people about the images?

Exercise 2: Biblical Titles for Jesus

- Working in pairs, see how many biblical titles for Jesus you can recall. Make a list: e.g. Comforter, Messiah, Lamb of God, Saviour, The Good Shepherd, Light of the World, Logos – there are about 200 titles in the New Testament showing how people saw Jesus.
- Compare lists in your group and see who has the most.
- Working in pairs, list all the titles for Jesus you can find in any hymn books, old and new, and how often each one is used.
- Why do you think some titles are more popular than others?
- What do modern titles for Jesus tell us about our faith today?
- Which is your favourite title, and why?

Exercise 3: Using Christmas and Easter Cards as Images of Christ

Ask people to collect Christmas and Easter cards, historical and contemporary, and from different parts of the world. Set them out on a display to be used in group work.

- Using the cards together with scripture passages, discuss the role of different characters in the story of the Annunciation and the Nativity. What impact did the coming of the Messiah have on them as reflected in the imagery? (Matthew 1.18—2.11; Luke 1.26–38, 2.1–21).
- Read the Magnificat (Luke 1.46–55). Do the images of Mary reflect the radical nature of her message?
- Select images that could be used to tell people who have little or no understanding of Christianity about the real meaning of Christmas and Easter.

St Richard's Prayer

Thanks be to thee, O Lord, Jesus Christ,
For all the cruel pains and insults
Thou hast borne for me;
For all the many blessings
Thou hast won for me.
O Holy Jesu, most merciful Redeemer,
Friend and Brother,
May I know Thee more clearly,
Love Thee more dearly,
And follow Thee more nearly. Day by day. Amen.

Handout 6
Continuing Programme for a Day Event or Part of a Course

The Power of Images

5 minutes: Introduction to the workshop.
10 minutes: Story 1: 'A Crucified African Christ'.
10 minutes: Story 2: 'The Barbed Wire Crucifix'.
30 minutes: Group discussion of the stories.
15 minutes: Break.

Working with One Image – Holman Hunt's *The Light of the World*

10 minutes: Introductory Talk: 'Holman Hunt and his Painting'.
30 minutes: Topics for discussion: Share in pairs.
20 minutes: Share in small groups.
15 minutes: Break.

The Power of Images

Story 1: A Crucified African Christ

A cold, wet, windy night was not the most auspicious start for working with images with an ecumenical Lent group in a small village community in north-east England. We met in the local church hall, bereft of any decoration except for some Sunday school offerings on a notice board. It says much for the commitment of the faithful that so many braved the elements and provided good cheer in such an unwelcoming ambience.

We took the events leading up to Christ's Passion as our theme for the course. After a short introduction the group was invited to choose an image from the display of pictures that was set out on tables round the room. Working together in small groups, the participants then took turns in talking about who Christ was for them in their chosen image. In one group, John, who had not said a word all evening, suddenly started to speak and, once he had begun, there was no stopping him.

John was dying of cancer. He knew he had not long to live but, imprisoned by his natural reserve, he had not been able to talk about his illness, let alone share his feelings or his faith. Neither his priest, his family, nor his close circle of friends could penetrate his defences. But that evening he had chosen a picture of a young, crucified African Christ crowned with thorns and, miraculously, he was released from his emotional captivity (see picture). For John, it was the peaceful face of the African Christ and its youthfulness that had pierced his heart. In contrast, he felt that he had had a good, long life and was now ready to die. For him, too, the serenity, which this image portrayed, gave him the assurance of eternal peace. With tears streaming down his face, John was at last able to share his innermost feelings about his coming death. A copy of the picture, fixed to the wall in his bedroom, gave him much solace during his last days.

10 – A Crucified African Christ

This was not the end of the story. As Holy Week approached, John was invited to join those having their feet washed at the Maundy Thursday service, a first in the village's Anglican church. Initially, he would have none of it. But after working with images of Christ washing his disciples' feet, he changed his mind. On Maundy Thursday he came forward with his fellow parishioners and duly had his feet washed. This was the last time he attended church. He died on Easter Monday. At his funeral, his priest told the story of how the image of a crucified African Christ had liberated John in his dying days, holding up the image for all to see. His grandsons were so moved by the story that they had to be given copies of the picture too.

John's story shows how powerful working with images of Christ can be. There is the initial impact, when an image seems to speak directly to you, unlocking your feelings and helping you to articulate and share your faith. But it doesn't stop there. Many people retain the image in their mind's eye, and experience an ongoing dialogue with it in the days ahead as it continues to work its transformation from within. All speak of being changed by the experience and of the joy in coming to a new understanding of their faith, however tentative and unstructured that may be.

For John, his chosen image not only helped him find peace during his last days, but it also inspired him to keep growing in faith, enabling him to confront new challenges with extraordinary good humour. His story has been told countless times. It greatly affected his family and friends, and it has also touched an ever-widening circle of strangers, like the ripples that emanate outwards when you drop a pebble in a pond.

Story 2: The Barbed Wire Crucifix

11 – The barbed wire crucifix, South Africa

This crucifix was originally made by a group of Roman Catholic youths in a church workshop in Johannesburg during the darkest days of the liberation struggle. Despite the fact that these African youngsters served regularly at the altar and sang in the church choir, they were hounded by the police – and a good number jailed. With the townships going up in flames, they just happened to be in the wrong place at the wrong time.

Huge rolls of barbed wire surrounded their homes in the townships outside the city, an ever-present reminder of military constraint and impending violence, symbolizing the siege mentality of the apartheid era. These Boer descendants had seemingly forgotten the enduring legacy of bitterness and hatred left by their erstwhile British enemies. Barbed wire had first been used during the Boer War to contain Afrikaner women and children in concentration camps, where hundreds died of disease and hunger.

Seventy years later, the barbed wire crucifix allowed this symbol of oppression to be transformed by Christ's suffering on the cross to become a subversive image, transcending time and space: offering the boys hope and courage in overcoming darkness and despair.

Moreover, this image has taken on a universal meaning, which speaks powerfully to people who have no knowledge of its past connotations but can identify with its liberating symbolism. In Britain it has been incorporated in the AIDS logo of Durham Diocese, while during a recent workshop with crosses in Winchester, Ann Lewin was inspired to write the following poem:[5]

Impaled

Created for protection,
how quickly you became
a symbol of oppression,
enclosing those
perceived to be a threat.
Barbed, razor wire
cutting our human kindness
to the quick.
Yet, hung on that wire,
Christ's body has become
the symbol of freedom.
The candle of hope*
burns brightly through
your barbs.

Ann Lewin

* *The Amnesty International candle is surrounded by barbed wire.*

Group Discussion

- What do the images in these stories mean to you?
- Are you inspired to write a poem or some sort of reflection?

Obviously, images of Christ are not only about pain and suffering. Many invite joy and celebration, comfort and trust, or an outpouring of love and devotion. What they have in common is the way we work with them. The different exercises have been designed to enable people of all ages and every walk of life:

12 – The candle of hope

- to discover Christ for themselves and experience him as a living reality;
- to get in touch with their innate spirituality and allow it to connect with their deepest feelings;
- to feel free to express their faith in ordinary everyday language, and to be confident in sharing it;
- to be enthusiastic about living their faith.

Introductory Talk: Holman Hunt and his Painting

Everyone should have a copy of this picture (or share one): readily available on postcards or the internet, in books, or personal copies. The image can also be projected onto a wall or screen from the CD-ROM.

Reproductions of William Holman Hunt's much-loved painting of Jesus in *The Light of the World* is found hanging in many homes and in stained-glass windows in churches. Hunt (1827–1910), who was born in Cheapside, London, received some formal training in art but became disillusioned with the contemporary scene. As one of the founders of the Pre-Raphaelite Brotherhood in 1848[6] he not only hoped to revitalize painting by close attention to detail and the use of vibrant colour, but also sought

13 – Christ's lamp from The Light of the World

to recover the spiritual qualities of medieval art. Coming from an evangelical background, and well versed in the Bible, his interpretation of Revelation 3.19–20, *The Light of the World* (1851–3), was the first of his religious works to bring him fame. Now in the chapel of Keble College, Oxford, it has been described as 'a sermon on canvas'. It was so popular that, with an assistant's help, he painted a larger version (1900–4), which toured the British colonies before ending up in St Paul's Cathedral. Another copy hangs in the Manchester Art Gallery.

Despite its familiarity, the dense symbolism in this image still offers a theological challenge. A bearded Jesus, clothed in a white seamless robe and patiently knocking at an old wooden door, is in reality knocking at the door of our hearts, inviting us to repent and let him in. The overgrown garden and the brambles obstructing Christ's way symbolize all that makes for personal sin, selfish greed and worldliness. Without a handle to the door, this gentle Jesus, who looks straight into our hearts, must wait patiently for us to admit him into our lives (cf. Matthew 7.7). But while the evangelistic message, reinforced by countless sermons, is soon trotted out, it is the imagery of the glowing lamp held by Christ that has a special meaning for folk in former pit villages. While it is said to represent the lamp of the Church, they say, 'It's like a miner's lamp, see.'

Although the pits no longer exist, mining still defines the life experience of these people and permeates their faith. Images of miner's lamps adorn Mothers' Union and trade union banners in the north-east; and a permanently lit lamp stands on the altar or hangs next to the aumbry holding the reserved sacrament in many churches. For them, Christ the Light of the World symbolizes hope. They believe that the light of Christ will overcome darkness, just as the miners' lamps did deep down in the pits, and that our Lord and Saviour will lead them safely through the many vicissitudes of life, as he protected the miners in their dangerous work.

Topics for discussion: Revelation 3.20

'Listen! I am standing at the door, knocking: if you hear my voice and open the door, I will come in to you and eat with you, and you with me.'

- Have you seen any of the original paintings?
- What strikes you most about this image?
- How does Hunt's depiction of Christian salvation coming to a sinful world affect your faith?
- Does the lamp have any special meaning for you ?

Share in Pairs

In pairs, spend 30 minutes discussing the questions given above. Make sure that you both have enough time to have your say.

Share in Small Groups

Gather together in small groups and share your response to this image.

- Have you gained any new insights?
- How did you feel about working with an image of Christ?

Handout 7
Worship with Symbols: Christ, the Light of the World

People should be seated in a circle with either a candle stand or sand tray in the centre. Each participant is given a candle or night-light, with matches to hand.

Chant	Worship can start with the singing of the Taizé chant: 'The Lord is my light, my light and salvation: in him I trust, in him I trust.'

Call to Prayer   A large candle is lit in the centre.

Leader   'You are the light of the world. A city built on a hill cannot be hid. No one after lighting a lamp puts it under the bushel basket, but on the lampstand, and it gives light to all the house. In the same way let your light shine before others, so that they may see your good works and give glory to your Father in heaven.' (Matthew 5.14–16)

Silent Reflection

JESUS SAID I AM THE LIGHT OF THE WORLD

14 – Jesus said, 'I am the Light of the World'

Sayings of Jesus

The Sayings are read slowly in turn by different participants, after which each one lights a candle or night-light and places it in the centre.

1   Jesus spoke to them saying, 'I am the light of the world. Whoever follows me will never walk in darkness but will have the light of life.' (John 8.12)

All   You are the light of the world.

2   'The light shines in the darkness and the darkness did not overcome it.' (John 1.5)

All   You are the light of the world.

3   'For all who do evil hate the light and do not come to the light, so that their deeds may not be exposed. But those who do what is true come to the light, so that it maybe clearly seen that their deeds have been done in God.' (John 3.20–1)

All   You are the light of the world.

4   Jesus said to them, 'The light is with you for a little longer. Walk while you have the light, so that the darkness may not overtake you. If you walk in the darkness, you do not know where you are going. While you have the light, believe in the light, so that you may become children of light.' (John 12.35–6)

All   You are the light of the world.

Penitence (the lighting of candles can continue after each refrain)

Leader	Lord, you breathed life and light into us.
All	But we allowed it to be overcome by darkness.
Leader	Lord, you lit your light in the heart of each person.
All	But we neglected to honour it.
Leader	Lord, you waited patiently to reveal your light to us.
All	But we did not welcome you into our lives.
Leader	God, who with his light revealed parts of ourselves which we did not have the courage to examine, may forgive us all.
All	Amen. Lord, have mercy.

15 – Lighted Candle

Prayers

O Christ, the Light of the World,
We thank you that your light shines among us.
Draw us ever closer to you,
So that free from sin
We may show forth the light of your glory in the world.
(Torres Straits, Australia)

Almighty God, grant that as we your children are bathed in the new light of your incarnate Word, so may that which shines by faith in our minds blaze out likewise in our actions. Amen. (Gregorian)

Leader	May the Lord send us out to broadcast his light of justice and wisdom to the ends of the earth: Father, Son and Holy Spirit.
All	Amen. Hallelujah.

Alternative worship is found in 'Light of Life. An order of service for Epiphany', Let All the World . . . Liturgies, litanies and prayers from around the world, compiled by Wendy Robins, 1990, London: USPG, pp. 17–23.

Notes

1 Translated by Mary H. Allies, 1898, London: Thomas Baker, reproduced in the *Internet Medieval Sourcebook*, ed. Paul Halsall, Fordham University Centre for Medieval Studies.

2 Leonide Ouspensky, 1978, *Theology of the Icon*, New York: St Vladimir's Seminary Press, pp. 9–10, 112.

3 Deborah Sheldon, 'Elected silence, sing to me', *Church Times*, 26 November 1999. See also her *Gospel Icons*, 1999, Cambridge: Grove Books.

4 Deborah Sheldon, *Church Times*, 1999.

5 © Ann Lewin, June 2010, 'Impaled' (used with permission).

6 More than 40 artists were associated with the Pre-Raphaelite movement including Holman Hunt, Edward Burne-Jones, Ford Maddox Brown, John Everett Millais and Dante Gabriel Rossetti.

2

ONE SAVIOUR FACING IN MANY DIRECTIONS

16 – Inuit (Eskimo) soapstone carving of the Madonna and children, Canada

One Christ: Many Christologies

Contextual theology is the theology that arises out of a particular historical context and addresses the concerns of that context. The Bible is a prime example of a contextual record. God's acts of redemption and liberation are narrated from the varying perspectives of those involved in the unfolding of salvation history. The Gospel writers are doing contextual theology when they draw on their own experiences and memories of Jesus to bring his message alive, but address quite different constituencies in their telling of the same basic story.

Indeed, all theologies are contextual, whether this is conceded or not, since all theological thinking is determined by the immediate context of those engaged in doing theology. However, contextual theology *per se* implies 'the *conscious* attempt to do theology from within the context of real life situations in the world'.[1] It is usually a communal effort, being grounded in the concerns of a specific group of people.

In different times and places people will ask different questions about their faith according to their historical, socio-economic, political and cultural contexts. This will give rise to unique theologies – Liberation Theology, Black Theology, Womanist Theology, Green Theology, Dalit Theology (of India), Water Buffalo Theology (in Thailand), etc. However, 'this does not deny the fact that faith as a commitment to God in Jesus Christ remains the same at all times and in all circumstances. In other words, while there is one faith, there can be different theologies.'[2]

The Incarnation is at the heart of contextualization. Christ of first-century Palestine takes flesh and is born anew within every tradition and context. As the Lord of history, he embraces all cultures yet transcends them all. While on earth, Jesus gave his disciples the freedom to speculate on his identity by asking: 'Who do you say I am?' (Matthew 16.13–20; Mark 8.29; Luke 9.18–21). This question may be paraphrased as: 'How do you see me in your specific context?' The range of possible responses is as wide as the range of people who are confronted by it. There are indeed as many theologies and Christologies as there are Christian traditions.

An image is not merely a representation of Christ, but an intrinsic revelation of the Incarnation. For instance, a Rembrandt or a Rubens is irrelevant to the *Heilsgeschichte*, history of salvation of the Masai in East Africa. To them, the only real Christ is the Masai Jesus: the Lion of Judah, portrayed as an African warrior (*The Christ We Share*, no. 6). He is both the elder brother of their ancestors and the elder brother of all humanity.

17 – Ethiopian Christ

Similarly, Jesus the Maori shaman in New Zealand is not just a symbolic embodiment of Christ, but a direct presentation of him in that particular context. In the glass etching of the Maori Christ in St Faith's Church in Ohinemutu, the traditionally robed figure appears to walk on the water of Lake Rotorua, beyond the window. For Maori people, this is not just Christ dressed as a Maori shaman, but Christ as he reveals himself to them: their very own Jesus. Through the Incarnation the particularity of Christ for each culture is brought together with his universality for all peoples, the images providing the connecting link.

Having developed their uniquely different contextual theologies, Christians around the world have needed to find new ways of worshipping God. Their prayers may sound odd to Westerners, because our liturgies are shaped by our context, but believers elsewhere may find our liturgies equally foreign, except that formerly they were conditioned to accept them as the norm. We need to be free to view Christ through imageries not our own and aspire to commune with him and our fellow Christians in a much more universal way.

Handout 8
Maori Lord's Prayer; and Programme for a One-off Occasion, Half a Day, or Part of a Full Day or Course

Refreshments provided as required.

Maori Lord's Prayer *(translated into English)*

Eternal Spirit, Earth-Maker, Pain-Bearer, Life-Giver,
Source of all that is and that shall be,
Father and Mother of us all,
Loving God, in whom is heaven,
May your sacred name echo through the universe.
The way of your justice be followed by the peoples of the world.
Your heavenly will be done by all created beings.
Your commonwealth of peace and freedom sustain our hope and come on
    earth.
With the bread we need for today, feed us.
In the hurts we absorb from one another, forgive us.
In times of temptation and test, strengthen us.
From trials too great to endure, spare us.
From the grip of all that is evil, free us.
For you reign in the glory of the power that is love, now and for ever. Amen.
(source unknown)

One Saviour Facing in Many Directions

	Maori Prayer or Denominational Worship
5 minutes:	Introduction.
20 minutes:	*Handout 9: Talk: 'The Many Faces of Christ over the Centuries'.*
30 minutes:	Bible study 2: John 10.1–18, The Good Shepherd.
30 minutes:	Exercise 3: 'Images of Christ over the Centuries'.
15 minutes:	Break.
30 minutes:	*Handout 10: 'The Received Christ versus the Indigenous Christ'.*
10 minutes:	Exercise 4: 'Titles for Christ in Other Cultures'.
10 minutes:	Exercise 5: 'Learning from Other Contexts and Cultures'.
45 minutes:	*Handout 11: Stories from Native American (First Nations) Peoples in Canada.*
	Story 3: 'The Arrival of the Magi', British Columbia, 1936.
	Story 4: 'The Apology of the United Church of Canada' 1985.
c. 15 minutes:	Group discussion. Variable.
	Handout 12: A Native American Liturgy with Symbols.

18 – Christ, Alpha and Omega

Handout 9
Talk: The Many Faces of Christ Over the Centuries

The process of translating the gospel into contemporary cultural forms has been going on since the beginning of the Christian era. Initially, the Word of God was translated into the flesh of Christ, within a particular social reality. The teaching of Christ was then contextualized in numerous Gospels from which our four, each with its unique stance, were chosen by the early Church as part of the Canon. With the spread of Christianity, the translation process expanded ever further, both transforming and being transformed by the receiving culture.[3] The people themselves generally took the initiative in drawing on indigenous thought patterns, imagery and symbolism to establish vernacular expressions of their new-found faith and to relate it to their everyday experiences.

In the translation process, *inculturation* is the term used to describe the symbolic exchange which takes place in the ongoing dialogue between the form in which the Christian faith is presented and the receiving culture. Each era in Christian history has produced new themes, depending on a variety of external factors. In a historical survey, the Dutch missiologist Anton Wessels argues that if the traditional religions were weak, they would eventually disappear. If they were deeply entrenched in the symbolic world of the receiving culture, elements of the old religion would be transformed by the incoming culture to meet new contextual needs and so become incarnated as indigenous expressions of Christianity.[4]

Symbolic images of Christ date back to the first century. Tertullian cites portrayals of the Good Shepherd on chalices. The oldest extant images of Christ the Good Shepherd are found in Rome from the third century on: in catacombs, on sarcophagi and grave slabs, and as an ivory statuette. Here, Christ appears as a slender, beardless young man surrounded by sheep or carrying a lamb on his shoulder. Although this motif has strong New Testament resonances (cf. John 10.14–15; Matthew 15.24; Psalm 23), the iconography is not initially Christian in origin but is drawn from the classical image of Hermes, protector of flocks, carrying a ram in his arms, and other images found on Etruscan artefacts. Early Christians reinterpreted this imagery to symbolize Christ as the Saviour who delivers us from sin and death, and promises eternal life (cf. Psalm 23). Similarly, early converts assimilated other elements of Greek and Roman mythology into their emerging Christologies.

In his masterly work on Jesus through the centuries, Jaroslav Pelikan maintains that in each age, 'the life and teachings of Jesus represented an answer (or, more often, the answer) to the most fundamental questions of human existence and human destiny, and it was to the figure of Jesus as set forth in the Gospels that these questions were addressed'.[5] Moreover, because each epoch posed different questions, the different portrayals of Jesus provide a key to the genius of the age. So, for example, Jesus becomes the Rabbi in first-century Judaism, the King of Kings in the Graeco-Roman context, and so on to the Historical Jesus in the eighteenth-century Age of Enlightenment, and the Poet of the Spirit in the art and literature of nineteenth-century Romanticism.

Modern European images of Christ illustrate the continuing process of inculturation except that the context is now unremittingly secular. In England, Stanley Spencer (1891–1959) exemplifies this process by setting the Gospel story in the cosy parochialism of his Thameside village of Cookham in Berkshire. *The Nativity* (1912) is re-enacted in a Cookham garden, *The Baptism of Christ* (1952) is set in a local swimming pool, *The Last Supper* (*c.* 1919) is crammed into a malthouse, while *The Raising of Jairus' Daughter* (1947) has a family group crowding the bedroom of a red-brick house. One of Spencer's most moving paintings is of *Christ Carrying the Cross* (1920) past his home in the High Street, followed by handymen balancing ladders on their shoulders, while onlookers hang gawping out of the windows. All are stolidly indifferent, except for Mary, who stands weeping. In the series of eight works depicting *Christ in the Wilderness* (1939–55), Spencer's Jewish Christ is modelled on Middle Eastern refugees in east London, while the flowers and animals of the Berkshire countryside evoke his belief in the goodness of God's creation and Christ's empathy with nature.[6]

Mark Cazalet and Dinah Roe Kendall are contemporary British artists who also incarnate Christ in everyday life. However, while Cazalet's dramatic paintings blend the figurative with the symbolic and the imaginary, Kendall sets her colourful depictions of the Gospel narratives in her surroundings, with family and

19 – The Good Shepherd, Kwa Zulu, South Africa

neighbours as active participants.[7] The Scottish sculptor, Peter Ball, is equally innovative in transforming driftwood into sculptures of the Madonna and Child, and crucifixes.[8]

Because inculturation is an ongoing process, expressions of the faith will continue to take new forms and imagery, whether this be in different parts of the world, or on the home front in council estates, multi-racial inner-city conurbations, rural communities or suburbia.

Bible study 2: John 10.1–18, The Good Shepherd

In Jesus' Galilee, there was a glut of messianic leaders only too eager to lead the Hebrew people. Full of ambition, they did not honour God's covenant with Israel. Jesus was the only one who was prepared to obey God's will and lay down his life for the people of God. The text warns us against false leaders and presents us with a model of godly leadership.

- List the qualities which you think are needed for a leader in a Christian community. Compare notes.
- In our society, young people in particular are easily lured into following the dubious morals of a celebrity culture. What message does the text have for Christians trying to cope with this situation?
- Argue, for and against, the proposition: 'The Good Shepherd as an image is patronizing towards the laity as leaders in the Church.'

Exercise 3: Images of Christ Over the Centuries

Find images of Christ from different eras and try and guess his title during that age, or make up your own – Rabbi (first century), Light of the World (second century), King of Kings (third century), Son of Man (fifth century), True Image (Byzantine icons, eighth and ninth centuries), Christ Crucified (Middle Ages, tenth and eleventh centuries), Man of Sorrows (thirteenth century), Prince of Peace (Crusades), Universal Man (Renaissance, sixteenth century), Teacher of Common Sense (Age of Enlightenment, eighteenth century), Poet of the Spirit (Romanticism, nineteenth century), Historical Jesus (twentieth century), Revolutionary (twenty-first century).[9]

Handout 10
Talk: The Received Christ versus the Indigenous Christ

20 – One-way missionary traffic

As the missionary movement gained momentum in the eighteenth and nineteenth centuries, the image of Jesus exported round the world was invariably Caucasian, no matter the culture of the indigenous people. The missionary zeal was to convert 'the heathen' to a European form of Christianity, inseparably linked to Western civilization and the racism that accompanied it. This precluded converts from honouring their Christ-ordained commission to evolve their own Christologies.

An imperial Christianity was matched by an imperial Christ, the kingly image becoming synonymous with dominance and triumphalism. Whereas the original concept of Christ the King was as liberator from all worldly tyrannies, Christ became the patron saint of conquistadores and colonizers, legitimating conquest and perpetuating subjugation. Such imagery, together with the gentle Jesus of Victorian piety, demanded resignation and submission in the face of oppression. Converts had no choice but to accept an other-worldly Jesus who had little relevance in their lives, and who was used to justify racial segregation and exploitation.

Missionary images of Christ remained deeply entrenched in the receptor cultures long after the colonizers had left, bequeathing a dualistic theology which separated the material from the spiritual, the body from the soul. God was kept firmly out of politics except when those in power invoked him to support the *status quo*, as in South Africa and the United States. It was a religion concerned with personal salvation and an interior moralistic faith divorced from the experiences of the wider community.

It was only in the closing decades of the twentieth century that the black consciousness movement gained momentum across the globe. As significant numbers of indigenous peoples began to protest against an oppressive missionary

21 – Navaho Christ

legacy, they consciously started to take responsibility for their religious freedom and to read the Scriptures with new eyes. What they found was fresh images of Jesus who took flesh in their context, their culture, and their historical experience.

In North America, the Sioux medicine man, Lame Deer, was one of those who railed against the prevailing European images of Christ:

> You have made a blondie out of Jesus. I don't care for those blonde, blue-eyed pictures of a sanitized, Chloroxed, Ajaxed Christ. How would you like it if I put braids on Jesus and stuck a feather in his hair? You would call me a very crazy Indian, wouldn't you? Jesus was a Jew. He wasn't a yellow-haired Anglo. I am sure he had black hair and a dark skin like an Indian. The white ranchers here wouldn't have let him step out with their daughters and wouldn't have liked him having a drink in their saloons. His religion came out of the desert in which he lived, out of his kind of mountains, his kind of animals, his kind of plants. You have made him into an Anglo-Saxon Fuller Brush salesman, a long-haired Billy Graham in a fancy nightshirt, and that is why he doesn't work for you any more. The trouble is not with Christianity, with religion, but with what you have made out of it. You have turned it upside down. You have made the religion of the protest leader and hippie Jesus into the religion of the missionaries, army padres, Bureau of Indian Affairs officials. These are altogether different religions, my friends.[10]

Lame Deer is not just protesting about some harmless white image of Christ, or even about a difference in cultural perspective. He is concerned about the socially and politically repressive components of the received tradition. This is well expressed in *The Road to Damascus: Kairos and Conversion*, a ground-breaking document in 1989, signed by Christians from seven countries – Namibia, South Africa, the Philippines, South Korea, El Salvador, Nicaragua and Guatemala:

> What we discovered was that Jesus was one of us. He was born in poverty. He did not become incarnate as a king or nobleman but as one of the poor and oppressed. He took sides with the poor, supported their cause and blessed them. On the other hand, he condemned the rich (cf. Luke 6.20,24) . . . He even described his mission as the liberation of the downtrodden (cf. Luke 4.18). That was the very opposite of what we had been taught. At the heart of Jesus' message was the coming of the Reign of God. We discovered that Jesus had promised the Reign of God to the poor.[11]

As Third World Christians found their voice in expressing radical new Christological insights, Liberation Theology in Latin America was followed by as many contextual theologies as there were countries of origin. This indigenous theological impulse was matched by imaginative portrayals of Jesus in every possible medium. These included a black, yellow and brown Christ clothed in worldwide national costumes, while being depicted as Liberator and Laughing Christ in the Americas; Freedom Fighter and Angry Christ in the Philippines; Smiling Christ in Korea; Black Messiah in South Africa; Rasta Jesus (Jesus is dread) in the Caribbean and United Kingdom; wise Guru in India; Christ the Workman in Hong Kong; Refugee in Uganda and Egypt; or Dancing Christ in Java.

The new Christologies have produced a style and form of art as radical as their theological content, while remaining rooted in the imagery of their cultural traditions. This kaleidoscope of images is illustrated in the garish clothing of the Calypso Christ from Jamaica; a Taiwanese crucifixion using laser art; the stippled rendering of the Road to Calvary by an aboriginal Australian; Christ the Enlightened One reflected in Buddhist iconography; a paper-cut Chinese nativity; or the resurrected Christ painted in Orthodox Ethiopian style on an ostrich egg.

The initial impact of these many faces of Christ can be quite shocking to anyone for whom the 'white' Christ is the norm. Western theologians are quick to warn about the dangers of 'syncretism'. They choose to ignore the fact that contextualization has been taking place in Europe over the last 2,000 years, and that discernment has

22 – The Transfiguration

always been necessary to sift out distortions in the inculturation process. This is not a modern theological phenomenon, nor is it culture specific. The transmutation of a Galilean Jewish Jesus to a blue-eyed Caucasian figure is a classical example of Christological syncretism.

Because the images come from different cultures, they can also be used in interfaith studies. Where Christianity is a minority religion, as in the East, characteristics of other faiths, deeply embedded in local traditions, will inevitably permeate portrayals of Christ. Indirectly, the images can sensitize us to the spirituality of other faiths, allowing us to see Christ from fresh perspectives. We are thus able to strip our inherited Christology of its Anglo-Saxon underpinnings and rediscover the Middle Eastern Jewish Jesus of the Bible, who died for the salvation of all humanity.

Exercise 4: Titles for Christ in Other Cultures

In different cultures and contexts Jesus has been depicted as: Teacher, Healer, Story Teller, Prophet, Guru, Shaman, Miracle Worker, Liberator, Freedom Fighter, Political Martyr, Refugee, Suffering Christ, Angry Christ, Black Messiah, Laughing Christ, Hollywood Hero, Christ the Mother, God's Fool, Worker Christ, Dancing Christ, Holy Child, the Good Shepherd (with different animals), Inner-City Christ, Gentle Jesus, etc.

- Find images to match some of the titles. Are there any difficulties in seeing Christ incarnated in other cultures?
- Images with a well-worn theme can be compared in different cultures so as to gain new insights, for example, the Nativity, the Good Shepherd, Christ with Children, Christ as Healer and Teacher, the Suffering Christ, the Road to Calvary and Crucifixion.

Exercise 5: Learning from Other Cultures and Contexts

Images of Christ from different cultures and contexts are set out on display

- as a way of learning about the worldwide Church;
- identifying with people in other cultures;
- being spiritually enriched by other experiences of the living Christ.

The group is divided into a number of small circles:

- Choose an image from an unfamiliar culture and meditate on it.
- After a time, ask people to say what influenced their choice of image. Discuss positive and negative aspects.
- What can we learn about Christ in different cultures and contexts?
- What aspects of Christ have been emphasized in the chosen images?
- How easy is it for us to receive a new understanding of Christ?

Handout 11
Stories from Native American (First Nations) Peoples in Canada

The first story, together with the liturgy, have been chosen to illustrate the process of inculturation in one particular culture. Sandwiched in between is the unprecedented Apology of the United Church of Canada to its indigenous peoples for having compromised their traditional beliefs and way of life in the name of Christ.

23 – The Arrival of the Magi

Story 3: The Arrival of the Magi, British Columbia, 1936

One of the earliest attempts at inculturation by Native American peoples in Canada was a painting by a young 'Red Indian' chief sent to the SPG by the Revd C. K. K. Prosser, and published in *The Mission Field* in April 1936. The missionary noted that water-colour painting was a new form of expression to the west coast people, as was the artist's use of indigenous symbolism to convey Christian teaching.

The tribal markings on the faces are similar to those on ceremonial dance masks, showing the rank and importance of the participants. The sacred dance was said to be 'the real art of these Indians', possessing deep religious significance. The painting, therefore, represents an occasion of great ceremonial and spiritual importance. According to the Revd Prosser,

The Virgin wears a chilkot blanket: both she and St Joseph by their dress show royal descent. The three chiefs come by canoe, the sea being the only highway. The canoes are of different types; thus the chiefs represent all mankind. The first brings a 'copper', a sort of Indian banknote, the symbol of wealth. The second brings a box containing the paraphernalia of certain dances. A man's rank and position are shown by the dances which he has the right to perform. This symbolizes honour. The third brings a 'talking stick', by which a man has the right to speak in council, the symbol of authority.

Painted in bright colours against a white background, the distinctive imagery in *The Arrival of the Magi* is still found in traditional forms of art and crafts in British Columbia today.

Story 4: The Apology of the United Church of Canada, 1985

In March 1985, Alberta Billy, a Native American woman from the tiny salmon-fishing community at Cape Mudge, on Quadra Island, British Columbia, made history at a General Council meeting of the United Church of Canada, the largest Protestant body after the Methodist and Presbyterian Churches united. Inspired by her grandfather's spirit, she bravely challenged the Church to apologize publicly for stripping her people of their spiritual symbols, in themselves potent images of Christ. A year later, at the next Council meeting, Moderator Robert Smith led the United Church in making a formal Act of Apology to their native congregations.

Long before my people journeyed to this land, your people were here, and you received from your elders an understanding of creation, and of the mystery that surrounds us all, that was deep and rich to be treasured.
We did not hear you when you shared your vision.
In our zeal to tell you the Good News of Jesus Christ we were closed to the value of your spirituality.
We confused western ways and culture with the depth and breadth and length and height of the gospel of Jesus Christ.
We imposed our civilization as a condition of accepting the gospel.
We tried to make you be like us and in so doing we helped to destroy the vision that made you what you were.
As a result you, and we, are poorer and the image of the Creator is twisted, blurred and we are not what we are meant by God to be. We ask you to forgive us and to walk together with us in the spirit of Christ so that our peoples may be blessed and God's creation healed.

A stone cairn was erected at Sudbury to mark the site of the Apology. It is in the shape of a circle, representing the unbroken circle of life, the prime symbol of the holistic native spirituality. However, it was deliberately left unfinished to symbolize the measure of the atoning work that was still expected of the Church. This continues to this day.[12]

This icon was designed by Bill Powless, of the Six Nations Reserve, in the 1980s, for the former Council on Native Affairs of the Anglican Church of Canada. It brings together many symbols of ancient meaning to native peoples in Canada, illustrating the role of inculturation in their striving for justice. These symbolic images have been incorporated within the liturgy.[13]

24 – Life In Its Fullness

Handout 12
A Native American Liturgy with Symbols

Quiet music may be played such as Native American flute music. Participants sit in a circle. Symbols are placed in the centre: a lighted candle, a standing cross, pine branches and large feathers are spread out on a blue cloth. The worship leader goes round the circle directing the smoke of burning sweetgrass or incense towards each person. Drawing it towards them, they offer it up in prayer to God ('For we are to God the aroma of Christ', 2 Corinthians 2.14). Images from the CD-ROM can be projected onto a wall or screen.

Call to Worship

Leader 1   O Great Spirit, whose voice is heard in the soft breeze and whose breath gives life to the world, we need your strength and wisdom. May we walk in beauty, may our eyes behold the red and purple sunset. Make us wise so that we may understand what you have taught us.

Leader 2   Help us to learn the lessons you have hidden in every leaf and rock. Make us always ready to come to you with clean hands and straight eyes, so when life fades, as the fading sunset, our spirits may come to you without shame. (Traditional prayer)

The Prayer of Six Directions

The group should face in the right direction as each prayer is said. Different leaders may be chosen to offer up the prayers.

We turn to the **east** and face the rising sun – God is praised for the gift of new life, of new days, of youth, of beginnings.
We turn towards the **south** – we give thanks for those people, events and things which warm our lives and help us to grow and develop.
We turn towards the **west** where the sun sets – we praise God for our sunsets, nights, for endings in our lives.
As we face **north** – we remember the challenges and difficulties in our lives.
We bend down to touch **mother earth** – and praise the Creator for the things which sustain our lives.
We look up to **the sky** – and thank God for our hopes and dreams.

All   Centred in the **Creator's universe,** we remember God's mighty deeds in our lives and thus move into the future.

The Antiphonal Responses

Leader   We are God's people within the eternal circle of life.
All   Truly, we are humanity together gathered from the six regions.
Leader   We take refuge under the outstretched branches,
All   from the powers and principalities of the world.
Leader   Behold the four white roots of the cosmic pine tree.
All   Rejoice that we are rooted deep into our mother earth.
Leader   We have overcome the darkness of pollution,
All   to welcome the green shoots of growth and hope.
Leader   We look for revelations and prophecies,
All   and for dreams and visions of Christ present throughout all creation.

First reading
Isaiah 52.13—53.5.

Prayer for the Healing of Creation

Almighty God, you bent the earth like a bow until it was one, round, shining planet. At your word the land was drawn into mountains and deserts, forests and plains; the waters were gathered together into rivers, lakes and seas. Many times when people crossed these seas from other lands they broke the circle of your creation by their greed and violence and shattered the lives of others. Renew the circle of the earth, O God, and turn the hearts of all your people to one another, that they and all the earth may live, and be drawn towards you in and through the power of your Son; who lives with you and the Holy Spirit in the circle of the Trinity: forever one God. Amen. (Source unknown)

A Navaho Litany of Penitence

I am ashamed before the earth;
I am ashamed before the heavens;
I am ashamed before the evening twilight;
I am ashamed before the blue sky;
I am ashamed before the darkness;
I am ashamed before the sun;
I am ashamed before the One standing within me who speaks to me.

The Absolution

Leader   May the pine tree, which is the tree of our ancestor Jesus, on which he died and rose again, grant us rebirth, forgiveness, and eternal life for ever.

All   Amen.

Second reading

Colossians 1.15–20.

Meditation: Story by Andrew Atagotaaluk of Pond Inlet, North West Territories

Many people in the North are soapstone carvers, and each carving carries the vision of the carver. If you were to see the stone before the carver touched it and gave it the life that it has, you would not be impressed. It is only a rough piece of stone, a chunk of unshaped rock. It is the carver who gives it the life that it has. Faith in Christ is like that. I believe that when you have such faith you are shaped by Christ to become what you really are inside yourself – just as the rock is shaped by the vision of the carver. The carver sees beyond the rough outer rock to the possible beauty of the carving. Each one is different from the next. Each has a life of its own and is a work of art. (*See Illustration no. 16*)

 This is how it is with life in Christ. You become more of what you are in your own culture . . . Each culture has its own beauty. Christ is the fulfilment of our culture, our language and our understanding of life. When we follow Christ, there is beauty in the image of who we are just as there is beauty in the carvings, which are carved in the vision of the carver.[14]

Reflect on the story in silent meditation.

Hymn

'When I needed a neighbour' (by Sydney Carter)

The Peace

Participants join hands in a circle as a sign of unity and solidarity.

Leader   Indeed, we have buried our arms and weapons,
All   may they lie buried forever for the peace of Christ.

People share the Peace with a handshake, hug or bow.

The Blessing

Leader   May Christ, the Bald Eagle, grant us freedom to soar in the blue sky of
             eternity.
All   Amen.
Leader   May Christ, the Salmon King, teach us to rise above all negativity.
All   Amen.

Leader	May Christ, the Mother Bear, make us valiant to resist all iniquity.
All	Amen.
Leader	And may the three-fold God – Father, Son and Holy Spirit – bless us with grace and serenity.
All	Amen.

Appropriate music is played while people sit in silence in quiet reflection.

Notes

1 Albert Nolan, Institute of Contextual Theology, n. d., p. 2.

2 Nolan, quoted by Larry Kaufmann, 'Good News to the Poor: the impact of Albert Nolan on Contextual Theology in South Africa' in McGlory Speckman and Larry Kaufmann (eds), 2001, *Towards an Agenda for Contextual Theology: Essays in Honour of Albert Nolan*, Pietermaritzburg: Cluster Publications, p. 7.

3 Andrew Walls, 1996, 'The Translation Principle in Christian History', *The Missionary Movement in Christian History: Studies in the Transmission of Faith*, Maryknoll: Orbis Books, pp. 22–7.

4 Anton Wessels, 1994, *Europe: Was it ever Really Christian? The Interaction between Gospel and Culture*, London: SCM Press (translated from the Dutch), pp. 3–15, 35–6, 47–54, 154–8.

5 Jaroslav Pelikan, 1987, *Jesus Through the Centuries: His Place in the History of Culture*, New York: Harper and Row, pp. 2–3, 220–31.

6 Timothy Hyman, n. d., *Stanley Spencer: The Apotheosis of Love*, London: Barbican Art Gallery catalogue; Timothy Hyman and Patrick Wright (eds), 2001, *Stanley Spencer*, London: Tate Gallery Publishing.

7 Dinah Roe Kendall, 2002, *Allegories of Heaven: An Artist Explores the 'Greatest Story Ever Told'*, London: Piquant.

8 Peter Ball, 1999, *Icons of the Invisible God*, Newark: Chevron Books.

9 Largely taken from Jaroslav Pelikan, 1987, *Jesus through the Centuries*, New York: Harper and Row.

10 Lame Deer and Richard Erdoes, 1973, *Lame Deer: Sioux Medicine Man*, London: Davis Poynter, p. 162.

11 *The Road To Damascus: Kairos and Conversion*, 1989, London: CIIR and Christian Aid, p. 8.

12 For further information see Janet Hodgson and Jay Kothare, 1990, *Vision Quest: Native Spirituality and the Church in Canada*, Toronto: Anglican Book Centre, pp. 144–52.

13 Used with permission of the Revd Donna Bomberry, Co-ordinator of the Anglican Council of Indigenous People, Canada.

14 This edited version is taken from Joyce Carlson (ed.), 1991, *The Journey: Stories and Prayers from People of the First Nations*, Toronto: Anglican Book Centre Publishing (earlier permission of First Nations Ecumenical Liturgical Resources, History and Publications Board). Andrew Atagotaaluk was elected the first Anglican (Inuit) Bishop of the High Arctic.

3

WORKING WITH IMAGES OF CHRIST

25 – Who do you say I am?

Working with images of Christ is all about liberating people to take responsibility for their own journey of faith. I start with a basic exercise which is the foundation for further programmes. Additional workshops can be added as needed and as time allows. The basic programme can be used on its own, with any size of group, as a one-off event, or as the start of a longer programme lasting a half or full day, a weekend, or longer course. I have even used it in the sermon slot during worship, allowing a little extra time.

Preparations: Display of Images, Seating and Timing

Preparing a Display

Before a workshop, time must be given to setting out a display of images from across the ages and around the world. Long, collapsible church tables are ideal. The bigger the group, the more images are needed. The tables should be well spaced around the sides of the venue so that participants can move freely between them without crowding. Standing exhibition panels are effective if the images can be peeled off and not too many people are involved.

In churches, one can spread pictures along pews, as well as on any accessible surface area – altar rail, side tables, chests, low windowsills, display cabinets, cupboards, tombs, etc. But restricted access needs careful management, and the images must be well lit and clearly visible. The vagaries of the congregation may also pose difficulties: during a service I have had parishioners sit on top of pictures because they were placed on their usual seats! Moveable chairs work better than pews as they can be arranged in different formations for group work.

Seating

Participants should sit in a circle to facilitate group sharing. A large group can be divided into a number of smaller groups of six to eight people, ten at the most. There is value in keeping a group such as a PCC together; but extra time must be allowed so that everyone can have their say. A relaxed atmosphere with comfortable seating and an equable temperature helps to create the right mood. If pews are used, then small groups of four to six people are bunched together in adjacent pews, with sharing taking place across the backs rather than along the lines.

Timing

This is flexible and depends on the overall length of the workshop, the number of people involved, and what manner of worship is envisaged. Participants should not feel rushed at any stage. It is also advisable to allow spare time to deal with any unexpected needs which require an immediate response. The approximate allocation of time should be announced at the start of each session.

26 – The Prodigal Son

Handout 13
Basic Programme and Opening Prayer for a One-off Event or Start of a Longer Programme for Working with Images

Refreshments as required.

'Who Do You Say I Am?'	
	Opening Prayer or Denominational Worship.
10 minutes:	Welcome, notices and introductions.
c. 20 minutes:	Session 1: Introductory Talk: 'Working with Images of Christ'.
5 minutes:	Optional dialogue by John Bell – 'Our Image of Jesus'.
10 minutes:	Session 2: Bible Study 3: 'Who do you say I am?'
10–15 minutes:	Session 3: Selection of One or Two Images – 'Who is Christ for Me Today?' Plus Meditation with chosen images.
c. 30 minutes:	Session 4: Sharing in Pairs – Sharing in Small Groups.
10–15 minutes:	Plenary session.
Variable	Worship with images.

Opening Prayer: Part of St Patrick's Breast Plate
(said or sung by all)

I arise today
Through a mighty strength, the invocation of the Trinity,
Through the belief in the threeness,
Through confession of the oneness,
Of the Creator of the Creation.

I arise today
Through the strength of Christ's birth with his baptism,
Through the strength of his crucifixion with his burial,
Through the strength of his resurrection with his ascension,
Through the strength of his descent for the judgment of Doom ...
Christ with me, Christ before me, Christ behind me,
Christ in me, Christ beneath me, Christ above me,
Christ on my right, Christ on my left,
Christ when I lie down, Christ when I sit down, Christ when I arise,
Christ in the heart of every man who thinks of me,
Christ in the mouth of everyone who speaks of me,
Christ in every eye that sees me,
Christ in every ear that hears me.

I arise today
Through a mighty strength, the invocation of the Trinity,
Through belief in the threeness,
Through confession of the oneness,
Of the Creator of Creation.[1]

Leader's Notes: The How and Why of Working with Images

(the fundamentals of which apply to further workshops)

Session 1: Introductory Talk – Working with Images of Christ

The leader gives some input as to what the images represent, with information about their historical, geographical, social, political and artistic content (see Chapters 1 and 2). The amount of information provided is determined by the purpose of the workshop. This is followed by a simple explanation of how the images are to be used throughout the programme:

- as a learning experience;
- as a way of doing theology together;
- to explore one's personal journey of faith;
- as an aid to prayer and meditation;
- sharing one's faith with others;
- bonding together as a group;
- enriching our worship by using images of Christ.

Optional Dialogue: John Bell – *Our Image of Jesus*[2]

I regularly use a dialogue devised by John Bell of the Iona Community to relax people and bring a fun element into the proceedings. Entitled *Our Image of Jesus*, it has two characters, one blustering and pompous and the other more down to earth and a little snide, providing contrasting views of how we should 'get our image of Jesus right'. The substance of the dialogue is meaty, but the way it is presented always raises laughs, especially if the incumbent in a parish group takes one of the parts.

Session 2: Bible Study 3 – 'Who do you say I am?'

This session starts with the reading of Peter's Confession of Christ, on which the workshop is based: 'Who do you say I am?' (Matthew 16.13–16; Mark 8.27–9; Luke 9.18–20). All three readings may be used, as they differ in nuance. A short theological reflection can be given by the leader before participants offer their own insights in a brief discussion.

27 – The Last Supper

Session 3: Selection of One or Two Images plus Meditation

Participants are invited to walk round the entire display and have a good look at all the images. This is an important part of the learning process and should be done slowly and quietly. Whatever the cultural background of people, the diversity of pictures can come as quite a shock, particularly if people are accustomed to thinking of Jesus as blond, blue-eyed and fair-skinned. Images of a suffering Christ may also be disturbing, and this should be mentioned beforehand. Participants are free to pick up the images to have a closer look or read any information on the reverse side. However, it is often better to ignore the artist's intention and let the images speak for themselves, giving free reign to the viewer's imagination, intuition and interpretation.

It must be emphasized that in no way are any of the images intended to be actual likenesses of Christ. A common mistake is to search for such an image. But each picture mirrors the artist's subjective imaging of some aspect of Jesus' persona, life, teaching or ministry. It may well reflect the artist's cultural background, or might even be abstract or symbolic.

After studying the display, participants are asked to choose one or two images in response to the question: 'Who is Christ for you at this very moment?' This can be challenging because of the range of images. Choosing two images allows for complementary or contrasting depictions of Christ. More than two involves too much time when it comes to sharing. People need to have an open mind and allow the images to speak to them before making their selection. Frequently, they are amazed at their choices: they may open up entirely new avenues of thought

28 – Symbols of Christ

and feeling, and the impact can be quite emotional. A box of tissues to hand is advised. Some people find it difficult to work with imagery, for theological or personal reasons. Others may have problems with anthropomorphic depictions of Christ or genuinely struggle to find an image with which they can resonate. This is where written words, texts, abstracts or symbolic imagery find their place.

People are asked to pick up their chosen images and return with them to their seats. Time is then given for silent meditation. This also allows slower participants to catch up without feeling under pressure. If two or more people want to work with the same image then they should sit together even if it means changing groups. Their different insights can be a creative experience.

Session 4: Sharing in Pairs – Sharing in Small Groups

Reflection on the images and ensuing discussion is focused on two questions:

- Why did you choose these images?
- Who is Christ for you as reflected in your chosen images?

In answering the first question, an image may have been chosen because it

- is artistically pleasing;
- is historically interesting;
- is familiar and has sentimental associations;
- resonates with a past or present experience;
- offers challenging new insights;
- provides an opportunity to learn about another culture and identify with new experiences;
- drew one to it for no obvious reason.

The second question is more difficult but also more important because it involves issues of faith and spirituality. The leader checks that everyone understands what is required of them and gives clarification where needed. It must be emphasized that the process is entirely open-ended with no right or wrong answers.

Sharing in Pairs

Sharing is initially done in pairs, encouraging trust and openness. A threesome may be formed if there are uneven numbers in a group, and they will require more time. People should feel free to say what they want and not be forced to go beyond their comfort zone. Clergy may need to be reminded that they have no special status: some find it difficult to abdicate control but they can learn much by listening. During a workshop, one priest heard members of his PCC discuss their personal beliefs for the very first time in 35 years in the parish.

The leader should not intrude upon private conversations, nor make any comment unless invited; but it is helpful to see what images have been chosen and to ensure that everyone has an equal chance to speak. People can reach surprisingly deep levels of intimacy in a short time, even with complete strangers. Paired sharing takes ten to fifteen minutes.

Sharing in Small Groups

The next step is for participants to form a circle, either in their small groups or in one big one. They then take turns in saying something about their chosen images in answer to the two questions. The leader may need to encourage the less confident or gently restrain the overly voluble. Again, people are free to share just as much as they wish, usually a summary of their paired conversation. If invited, a partner can assist in recalling important insights.

After each participant has spoken, their images are placed on the floor in front of them, so building up a collective picture of who Christ is for the group as a whole. The larger the group, the longer it will take to complete the exercise. Time is then given for people to reflect on their combined display of images. It is good to identify any common themes such as suffering, reconciliation, comfort or celebration; and to discuss briefly the implications of this for the group.

Plenary Session

The group comes together as a whole and is given an opportunity:

- to reflect on their experience;
- to offer any comments about the images;
- to ask any questions;
- to evaluate what they have learned from the exercise;
- to be warned about confidentiality: that which has been shared should not be discussed afterwards.

Leaders must remember that working with images is about affirming people in exploring and sharing their faith, and that this may well be a somewhat disturbing new religious experience. Some clergy cannot resist offering a homily at the end of a workshop, nervous that the formularies of the Church might have been transgressed. But an authoritarian leadership model puts paid to any further open discussion. However, there is real value in clergy getting together later with members of their group to evaluate the exercise. It is also useful for participants to report back to their congregation either in a magazine article or during a service.

Worship with Images

At the end of the workshop, participants are asked to bring their chosen images to the place of worship, whether this be a church, chapel, or the workshop venue itself. If the latter, then it is good to rearrange the chairs so as to create a different atmosphere. The images are laid out on the floor in the shape of a cross, or a few

29 – Christ washes his disciples' feet

little crosses, so as to be visible to all. This is a powerful focus for worship, bringing together all that has been shared during the course of participants' time together.

Depending on the time of day, worship can take the form of Morning or Evening Prayer, Compline, a Eucharist, or any other denominational service. The Wild Goose Community in Iona has produced *A Wee Worship Book* (1989), which provides a range of alternative liturgies with a Celtic flavour. This material can be reproduced freely for a one-off occasion and participants are encouraged to lead the worship. Alternatively, a liturgy has been composed for our purpose (see end of chapter).

Participants may also compose their own liturgy, making it truly 'the work of the people'. Sufficient time must be allowed to allocate different tasks to small teams of people. Smaller numbers can work in pairs and do more than one task. They need to take responsibility for:

- overseeing the organization and content of the worship, and ensuring that everyone knows what is expected of them and when;
- arranging the seating, setting out the images, and decorating the worship space with flowers, greenery or candles, as desired;
- choosing a greeting for the start, a blessing at the end, and deciding on how the Peace will be shared;
- choosing songs or hymns and providing music, live or recorded, which can be played at the beginning, during the prayers, and at the end;
- selecting appropriate Bible readings;
- composing their own prayers and/or selecting some from resource books. Time should be allowed for silent meditation on the images and for people to offer up their own petitions;
- Optional – using drama such as one of John Bell's meditations: 'He was in the World', a spoken reflection on the life of Jesus.

Resource material should be made available, such as Bibles, prayer manuals, printed liturgies (for all seasons and from around the world), hymn and song books with music, a standing cross, candles, incense, drapery, large sheets of paper and felt-tip pens. The order of service can be written up or projected for all to see so as to avoid confusion.

Handout 14
Programme for Additional Workshops for a Longer Event

There can be a break for refreshments between each session. If there is a lunch break before continuing, then the group might choose to celebrate Holy Communion before lunch.

'Worship with Images' could be left until the end of the day's programme, and images then used from one of the following two workshops.

Who Am I In Christ?

15 minutes:	Select one image for 'Who am I in Christ?'
15 minutes:	Silent meditation.
15 minutes:	Optional sharing in pairs – some people choose to remain in meditation until the end of the exercise.
15 minutes:	Optional sharing in small groups, placing images on the floor as before. *(No plenary session.)*

This exercise is very personal, hence the need for some to remain in silent meditation throughout. In selecting an image, one might see oneself as either a Mary or a Martha, contemplative or active, or a bit of both. Or one might identify with the disciples, feeling fearful of being tossed around in a stormy sea, one's life seemingly out of control. Others have felt a positive sense of calling as a disciple, or of being sent out by Christ. Yet others have grappled with images of the rich young man, the woman taken in adultery, Zacchaeus taking refuge up a tree, or of experiencing 'the dark night of the soul' with Jesus in the wilderness. One bishop chose the picture of Doubting Thomas, while another agonized over Peter's betrayal. All have found it an extremely powerful experience which has remained with them long after the workshop.

A break is advised before continuing with the next session, which, in complete contrast, is communal and allows participants to take a more active role.

Who is Christ for your Church or Fellowship Group?

10 minutes:	Session 1: Select an image that reflects how you think Christ is experienced in your church or group at present.
10 minutes:	Session 2: Select an image that reflects how you would like Christ to be experienced by the church or group in the future.
10 minutes:	Sharing in pairs – optional.
30 minutes:	Group sharing: compare the difference between the two chosen images.
15 minutes:	Plenary session: what does this mean for our faith group?

In a longer programme, worship then follows. Images can be used from either one of the two workshops instead of the first basic one.

Handout 15
Responses to the Workshops

Story 5: 'Seeing Our Faith' in North-East England

Stephen Conway, former Archdeacon of Durham and now Bishop of Ely, recalls a day workshop for his Tees Valley PCC in 1999. A neutral venue was chosen, about 20 miles away from home, in the hope that this would be a bonding experience for the leadership group. The purpose of the image workshop was to break some of the traditional clergy dependency and to give a voice to those who rarely participated in regular meetings. As Bishop Stephen recollects:

30 – *The Good Shepherd*

> Everyone joined in willingly. The images were varied, and I was intrigued to see what people would choose. One person was an artist and she chose striking abstract images. Most PCC members, however, opted for strongly realistic images. Not everyone picked traditional images; but most did. Of course images of the Cross were chosen, while some were drawn to 'soft' images of Jesus as Shepherd and as the Saviour, who suffers little children to come to him. As each person described his or her response to their chosen images, even the shyest member was unusually eloquent. Those not known for being very reflective in public were able to be perceptive both about their images and their own faith journey.

> The exercise was productive on a number of fronts. It certainly met the objectives which had been agreed beforehand. It further illustrated very clearly for me the importance of the humility required of priests and all those in Christian leadership to empty a space for others to grow into. It demonstrated the value of lay leadership in nurturing the people of God.

> The Images workshop is also the place where our assumptions of our spirituality can be safely reviewed and then safely challenged. It did not leave any of us in the same place. We all moved on, not only in our relationship to Christ but in our relationships with each other. We already cared for each other; but we learned that we could still surprise one another and deepen our respect for each other. Council meetings were never the same again!

In any workshop in the north-east, there was always a strong preference for images of Jesus with children and animals, The Good Shepherd, the Suffering Christ, and for Holman Hunt's *The Light of the World*. In the West we are accustomed to anthropologists analysing the religious beliefs of indigenous peoples in other parts of the world. But for an English regional community to have its corporate spirituality described in similar terms came as something of a shock. As Bishop Stephen said:

> Why should we be shocked? In fact, it was most helpful to think about the pastoral and caring spirituality of the north-east, expressed in favoured images of Christ as gentle Shepherd and the welcomer of children. At first sight, one might think that the fit was odd. After all, the communities of the region have gone through so much hardship that people have had to learn how to be tough and self-reliant through poverty, through hard physical labour and through long-term unemployment. It is precisely this unrelenting environment, however, which draws us to warm and accepting images of the Lord. People know a lot about the Cross in their own experience. Traditionally, communities have been held together by resilient women who have provided mutual support and loyal care. The Lord who is the source of that embrace draws us in. More challenging images can be left over from the struggle of living and loving.

Story 6: 'Seeing Our Faith' in South Africa

In the small village where I live, a group of ten to fifteen people met regularly together in our local retreat centre for many months. We worked with a variety of images, some being thematic, others following the liturgical year. Only a few of the group were churchgoers. All had had some or other denominational connection in times past, but most had severed any formal ties years ago for a variety of reasons. In addition, visitors were welcomed including Jews, Buddhists, a Sufi, a number of New Agers, and a member of the Findhorn community from Scotland. They came out of interest, and their questions challenged us to explore our faith more deeply and to relate it to our daily life. All our meetings were celebrated with homemade bread and soup. This being a wine-growing area, the wine flowed freely – a true agapé fellowship.

For most of the group, the initial reaction to the images was one of surprise: surprise at being confronted by a multicultural Christ, surprise at

31 – Christ Walking on Water

the differences in people's responses, and surprise at the honesty and profundity of the theology that emerged. Said one, a trained counsellor:

> The visual impact is so powerful that you can get in touch with your feelings just by looking and being given time to take it all in. The images go straight to the heart. You are seeing instead of someone talking or reading, so that your mind doesn't get in the way. It helps that you don't have to justify your choice of picture, just let it speak to you. The images are very personal and made me feel very emotional, especially those that had anything to do with children or were about love. People, especially the older generation, are generally frightened of going internally and try avoiding it. But the power of the visual helps to make that connection.

This friend was particularly struck by the therapeutic potential of the imagery. Another member, a Roman Catholic, was an experienced Jungian analyst, and he continually highlighted the shadow side of Christ in the images. He encouraged us to acknowledge the repressed hidden part of ourselves, to bring it to the surface and integrate it so that as people we might become whole.

A potter in the group saw the images as a wonderful way of learning because of their ability to involve people who were shy or diffident about sharing something of themselves. Obviously some people do get stuck, locked in by their inhibitions. But what impressed her most was 'the hidden way' in which the images called out an emotional response. This friend has an Anglican school background but sees herself as an agnostic who is struggling to fathom the mystery of life:

> Why I chose a particular picture, why it spoke to me, told me a lot about myself. It was also fascinating listening to how pictures around the same theme, or even identical pictures, talked to different people. We were a varied group and quite unselfconsciously they shared much about who they were and how they thought. I also loved the way the images portrayed Christ in a new light, the new insights this gave me. The images freshened the whole story of Jesus because they were so different, bringing it all alive. The black images in particular gave me a whole new and unexpected perspective.

One picture that has remained with her was of the Last Supper. It was set in a market place with crowds standing around an inn. She recalls:

> It was all so human. The pictures tell us so much about the human condition. The emphasis put on religion is so often divorced from the everyday things of

life. Too often the Church tries to contain and grab the story to itself. Dogma closes people off and they opt out rather than confront it. But the Jesus story is so universal. It speaks to anyone, whoever and wherever they might be.

Handout 16
Exercises with Images

These are ideal for any fellowship group, whether for a one-off occasion or part of a longer programme. Each takes about half an hour.

Exercise 6: Selection of Images

- How many tried to find an image of Jesus as he might have looked in first-century Palestine? Was this unimportant for others?
- How many chose an image which emphasized Jesus' earthly ministry such as healing or teaching? Why?
- How many chose a white Jesus, or otherwise specifically looked for an image from another culture? Why?
- How many chose an image of Jesus suffering? Why?
- How many chose an image which was either abstract, symbolic or used words? Why?
- Does it matter that people see Jesus in different ways?

Exercise 7: Images that Challenge

Choose an image which is problematic for you in some or other way:

- Identify the nature of the problem – indifferent art; unedifying portrayal of Christ; too sentimental; too abstract; cultural problems (Asian or African); racial problems (black or brown); theological difficulties; as a female figure or refugee; in unfamiliar situations (suffering in war or prison, as an angry Christ, living with AIDS, smoking a cigarette, dancing or partying, as a football player, etc.).
- Share the nature of your difficulties in pairs.
- How could such an image enrich your understanding of Christ?

Exercise 8: Using a Limited Number of Images

About ten contrasting images are fixed on walls or screens around the room. After looking at all the images stand next to the one of your choice. Each group then spends time sharing their reasons for their choice. Anyone on their own teams up with another loner to discuss their respective choices. Group discussion then follows:

- What images were most popular, and why?
- What images attracted little interest, or were ignored, and why?
- Is there any discernible sense of a corporate spirituality, for example a loving, protective Christ; one who suffers; one who challenges, etc.?
- If so, what does this say about who we are, and how we live our faith?

Working with images can provide a good foundation for catechetical teaching and spiritual training, but careful listening must come first. People's concerns, doubts, anxieties and fears all surface in workshops. At the same time, giving people space in which to do theology for themselves, rooted in their own experience, is at the heart of our God-given mission. This is what makes our journey in faith both contextual and incarnational.

Handout 17
Liturgy: 'Who Do You Say I Am?

Leader	Come let us gather in the Temple with Anna and Simeon,
All	to welcome the Lord.
Leader	Why is he the Lord?
All	Because he became a servant to free us from bondage.
Leader	Who do you say I am?
All	You are the Messiah born of the womb of Mary.
Leader	Who do you say I am?
All	You are the one to whom the wise men around the world came to pay homage.

32 – Who do you say I am?

Reading

Philippians 2.5–8.

Leader	You assumed our humanity but we failed to recognize you.
All	Lord, have mercy.
Leader	We nailed you time and time again to the cross.
All	Christ, have mercy.
Leader	Holy Spirit, you created life but we desecrated it.
All	Lord, have mercy.
Leader	May the Lord forgive you and me.
All	Amen.

Hymn

'When I survey the wondrous cross'.

Meditation: The Conversion of Sadhu Sundar Singh

Sadhu Sundar Singh was born in India, in September 1889, into a pious Sikh family. He was sent to a mission school where he encountered the Christian faith for the first time. He resented the way the missionaries denigrated his religion and culture as they preached the gospel. Inevitably, the teenage Sundar came to identify Christianity with colonialism. His animosity towards the Eurocentric Jesus as portrayed by the missionaries eventually led him to burn a copy of the Bible in the market square.

That very night, Sundar had a vision of Christ in which he said, 'My child, why do you crucify me?' Like St Paul before him, Sundar repented and accepted Jesus as his Saviour. He spent the rest of his life as a penniless monk preaching the crucified Jesus of his vision. Sundar understood Jesus as the Messiah suffering in the image of the poor of the world. Sundar became known as the Sadhu (saint in Sanskrit). The Sadhu taught Christians around the world to pray through silence and contemplation rather than using too many words.

Reading

Matthew 25.31–46

The group reflects on the Gospel reading in silence.

Leader	Who do you say I am?
All	You are the one who hung on the cross for us.
Leader	We meet Jesus in the image of the poor and the persecuted,
All	as we serve and care for the least among us.
Leader	We come face to face with Jesus,
All	as we encounter him in the image of the last and the lost.
Leader	Who do you say I am?
All	You are the one who rose from the grave, conquering death.
Leader	Who do you say I am?
All	You are the one who commissioned Mary of Magdala to preach the good news to the apostles.
Leader	Who do you say I am?
All	You are the prophet of the Kingdom of God.
Leader	The risen and ascended Jesus bless us and keep us,
All	even the Messiah made in the image of God. Amen.

Hymn

'Thine be the glory'.

33 – Historic French Canadian Christ

Notes

1 This hymn is contained in the ancient Book of Armagh. Although the original Old Irish lyrics were traditionally attributed to Saint Patrick in the fifth century, it was probably written a few centuries later: see http://www.en.wikipedia.org/wiki/Saint_Patrick's_Breastplate for the full version.

2 John Bell, 1995, *He Was in the World*, Wild Goose Resource Group, Glasgow: Wild Goose Publications, pp. 69–70.

4

RE-IMAGING MISSION

34 – Behold My Hands and Heart

Introductory Talk: A New Way of Doing Mission

Working with images of Christ across the world has proved to be a profound spiritual experience for an amazing cross-section of people. The multiracial, intercultural and ecumenical dimensions have been significant, but the response of lay people has been even more surprising. Like the woman with the flow of blood (Luke 8.43–48), many do not consider themselves worthy to encounter Christ face to face. Yet using images endows them with the courage to develop a personal faith, instead of an unquestioning acceptance of the received formularies of the Church. Too often these are enshrined in an incomprehensible diet of doctrine and dogma, while worship can degenerate into right behaviour – when to stand, sit, kneel, genuflect, find the correct page, and say the right responses. Not only does this reinforce a chronic dependency of laity on clergy, but it fails to address people's spiritual needs. They may well be the mainstay of the church, doing good works, fund-raising, and so forth; but their faith may never have been brought to life in a transformative experience.

Laurie Green, a Church of England Bishop, cites graffiti on a theological college wall to illustrate just how intimidating the intellectual approach can be: 'Jesus said to them, "Who do you say that I am?" They replied, "You are the eschatological manifestation of the ground of our being, in which we find the ultimate meaning in our interpersonal relationships." And Jesus replied, "What?"'[1]

Working with the images is rooted in a unique theology of mission which values people for who they are, enabling them to unburden themselves of restrictive Church teaching and rediscover and articulate their faith in their own words. Moreover, the images offer a radical new way of reflecting on faith in relation to contemporary life, encouraging people to be more outward-looking, and to grapple with a broader range of issues. For many people, it is a brave move to do theology as members of a community of faith, without having to walk the tight-rope of doctrinaire God-talk. In using images, they can experience an uninhibited freedom as they become enthused with the Spirit of God. Mission is a natural move forward as they look to see where God is already active in the world and are motivated to join in.

35 – The Woman of Samaria

Handout 18
Programme for Moving into Mission with Images and Mission Prayer from Zaire

Stand alone or part of a longer programme following on from the Basic Exercise in Chapter 3. Refreshments as required.

Moving into Mission with Images

	Mission Prayer From Zaire
5 minutes:	Introduction.
10 minutes:	Introductory Talk: 'A New Way of Doing Mission'.
15 minutes:	*Handout 19: Talk: 'Journeying in Faith'*.
Variable:	Exercise 9: 'Sharing a Personal Image of Christ'.
20 minutes:	Exercise 10: 'Reflecting On Our Own Journey of Faith'.
15 minutes:	Break.
20 minutes:	*Handout 20: Talk: 'Re-imaging the Context for Local Mission'*.
Variable:	Exercise 11: 'Who is Jesus for Those Around Us?'
Variable:	Denominational Worship if appropriate.

Mission Prayer from Zaire

O God, enlarge my heart that it may be big enough to receive the greatness of your love,

Stretch my heart that it may take into it all those who with me around the world believe in Jesus Christ,

Stretch it that it may take into it all those who do not know him but who are my responsibility because I know him,

Stretch it that it may take in all those who are not lovely in my eyes and whose hands I do not want to touch;

Through Jesus Christ, my saviour. Amen. (Source unknown)

Handout 19
Talk: Journeying in Faith

Images of Christ are particularly useful in pre-evangelism, or for awakening a dormant faith, as in preparing people for baptism, whether a child or an adult. The late Sheila Day, in Billingham in the north-east of England, used images as a way of drawing out what adults already know or feel about Jesus, helping them to own the discussion from the start. Apart from the usual favourites of Jesus with children and animals, or *The Light of the World*, the photo of Robert Powell as Jesus of Nazareth in the television series (*The Christ We Share*, no. 27) was very popular, as were Christmas nativity scenes, prayer cards and crosses. Parents were also encouraged to use pictures when talking to older children.

As part of the journey of faith, the next step is to encourage people to use images in a workshop. Many who have never talked about Christ before continue to do so long afterwards, and are then eager to learn more. Sometimes, the images have so deeply affected their lives that they have wanted to share their new-found feelings in the strangest places – a railway station, dress shop, in the street – and this can be an emotional experience.

In a parish context, Alison White was fascinated to see who came to a workshop: some came out of curiosity, some from habit, some because they knew they were spiritually hungry for the visual.[2] She was deeply moved by people's openness and generosity in exploring and sharing their responses to the images and, for many, their *need* to do so. In a verbal church culture, people commented on how rare it was to be given a 'language' in which they felt at home and fluent.

For many clergy, working with images has enriched their prayer lives, revitalized their preaching, given them valuable insights into where people are coming from, and rejuvenated their ministry. A rural dean came to a fresh sense of his priestly vocation through meditating on an image of Peter receiving the keys of the kingdom of heaven (Matthew 16.19), while a picture of Christ in the wilderness inspired a parish priest to become a spiritual director. All-clergy groups favour Salvador Dali's picture of *Christ of St John of the Cross* (1951), with the crucified Christ looking down on the world from above. Its familiarity offers safety. Braver souls choose more challenging images such as the woman taken in adultery, the rich young ruler, or the disciples asleep in the Garden of Gethsemane.

In Wales, an elderly bard chose *The Tortured Christ*, showing a skeletal Christ doubled up in agony on the cross. The sculpture is by the Brazilian artist Guido Rocha, who had survived being wrongfully imprisoned and severely tortured. He associated his suffering and that of fellow prisoners with the agony of Christ, and wanted to express his belief that God's grace overcomes all evil (*The Christ*

36 – The crucifixion

We Share, no. 2). Many people have used this image to pray for the plight of oppressed people. The Welsh bard, however, had terminal cancer and he associated Christ's agony with his own torment of pain. In sharing his experience with his colleagues, he found release in an outpouring of poetry in his native tongue.

Alison White's experience in a theological college was that often people struggled to make connections between a new world of academic theology and the more familiar realm of personal faith.[3] Working with images enabled ordinands to find a language with which to reflect on their choice of picture, sharing in ways that were unselfconsciously enriched by their studies. She believes that had they started with theological text only they would have missed developing the capacity for theological reflection in its truest sense. It also influenced their formation by helping them to engage with their whole selves, not just their intellect.

My experience with ordinands had unexpected results. In selecting images for who they thought Christ was for their theological college, five groups whittled their pictures down to almost identical images. These showed symbolic representations of a fragmented Christ with sharp points protruding at every angle. In discussion, the ordinands claimed that while the college projected a perfect image to the outside world, their experience was of tension and lack of trust. They confessed to suppressing their uncertainties and problems for fear of being found wanting. Two women left the room in tears. The Principal was advised of some of the issues that had arisen, and a counsellor was appointed soon afterwards.

Exercise 9: Sharing a Personal Image of Christ

People are invited to bring one or more of their own images of Christ – paintings, postcards, pictures in a book, crosses or crucifixes, etc. The local library is a useful resource. Sitting in a circle, participants take turns sharing:

- Why the image/s are important to them.
- Who Christ is for them in the image.

(This is a good way of getting people to share their personal faith story.)

Exercise 10: Reflecting On Our Own Journey of Faith

Choose an image of 'Who was Christ for me as a child – or before my confirmation, ordination, marriage, or other significant event?'

- Allow time to meditate on the image.
- Share in pairs.
- Compare your image with the one/s chosen in the basic exercise. Identify any significant changes in your faith over time:
  - Do you think the changes signify a growth in faith?
  - If so, what form has this taken?
  - If you have chosen a similar image over time, do you think you need to move on?

Handout 20
Talk: Re-imaging the Context for Local Mission

In local mission it is important to first identify the context where God is already at work so that your planning, whether it is for just being available and supporting people with prayer, or for actively doing something, is appropriate. Two quite different uses of imagery illustrate the range of possibilities in getting a feel for the situation.

The village of Whalton, Northumberland, celebrated the Millennium by giving each resident a disposable camera to record their favourite images. A local artist, Ian Johnson of Broomhill, then cut out small sections of the photos to produce a montage of the face of Christ, 6ft by 4ft 6in, which is on display in the twelfth-century parish church of St Mary Magdalene. The collage consists of 2,850 individual pieces and includes stone walls, gates, gardens, trees, fields, post boxes, road signs, animals and birds of every description, bicycles, cars,

37 – Whalton Christ

tractors, houses, the church, children, couples, in fact everything that makes for community and the natural world in which it is set. It is a classic example of how a lay Christian was inspired to see the face of Christ in and among the people of God and his creation. In so doing, God becomes a reality in our lives, a visible image of the Body of Christ accessible to all, as well as providing excellent groundwork for local mission.

In a completely different context, an extended workshop was held for the Diocese of Portsmouth in their Anglican Cathedral of the Sea, in spaces where art and images reflect the maritime influence on the life of the Mother Church. This much influenced the participants' response in focusing on *Who is Christ for you? Who is Christ for your church? Who is Christ for the Diocese of Portsmouth?* As Jeremy Dussek, a former parish priest in Fareham, recalls, people from across south-east Hampshire and the Isle of Wight were challenged to discover in the images of their ports, rivers and seascape, the Messiah who meditated, preached, fished and even slept on boats plying the Sea of Galilee.

Those from Fareham Deanery reflected on images of sailing boats, reminding them that Saint Birinius brought Christianity to the town in AD 634; and that they are called to leave their safe harbours, taking their faith to 'new' towns springing up round about. The recent rise of the Spinnaker Tower in Portsmouth, and the long-established Needles Lighthouse, were reminders of the Church's vocation to relight the flame on the lamp stand and bring hope to people struggling with the demands of contemporary life. The concerns of those living inland were dominated by the major new A3 road-building project. At the end of the day, the images selected were offered to God in support of the diocese's planned *Kairos* mission.[4]

38 – Salmon-fishing boat at sea – from a stained-glass window, United Church, Cape Mudge, Quadra Island, British Columbia

Exercise 11: Who is Jesus for Those Around Us?

This exercise involves listening to how different people see Jesus:

- What do people you know say about Jesus – family, friends, people at church, workmates, non-Christians, former churchgoers, etc?

Your findings provide a foundation for mission in your local context.

Handout 21
Programme for Looking Outward in Mission – Making a Visual Mission Statement

Making a Visual Mission Statement

10 minutes:	Introduction: the leader explains the purpose of the process.
10 minutes:	Choose one image in response to the following question:

'How would your Image of Christ serve as a Visual Mission Statement for your church or fellowship group?'

10 minutes:	Meditate with the image in silence until all are ready.
15 minutes:	Defend your choice of image in your cluster with as much passion as possible.
15 minutes:	Each cluster must select just one of their images to serve as their agreed *Visual Mission Statement*. Animated debate is encouraged as the images are gradually whittled down.
Variable:	A spokesperson from each cluster reports back on their final selection, and on how this decision was made.
Variable:	The clusters then vie with each other to get their particular image chosen as *the* visual mission statement for their church or fellowship group as a whole.

Preparation

A wide range of images of Christ is set out on display as before. The group is divided into clusters of three or four, who remain together throughout the session.

Leader's Notes: Making a Visual Mission Statement

This method requires participants to move from a quiet inner reflection on personal faith, as in the Basic Exercise, to thinking about a corporate spirituality, which looks outward in mission. Participants are also encouraged to actively defend their faith in order to gain greater confidence in expressing their beliefs in a supportive environment. This is an excellent starter for evangelism, while the fun element is integral to the experience. Every participant is asked to select an image which for them encapsulates the mission intention of their faith community, be it their church, a Bible study or house group, a confirmation class, youth group, lay ministers' fraternal, shared ministry team, Mothers' Union, HIV/AIDs support group, prayer fellowship, prison or student chaplaincy, etc.

The chosen image needs to be readily understood by everyone, especially those with little or no knowledge of Christianity, without any explanation. The aim is to communicate God's love and concern for people through non-verbal imagery that is as relevant to those both inside and outside the Church. Passion is a crucial element in the process as each participant defends his or her choice of image: we are now moving from faith-sharing to apologetics, from empathetic listening to a vigorously reasoned defence of the Good News as embodied in an image of Christ. Whereas most people struggle to define mission, imagery provides a non-threatening way of expressing one's thoughts.

The dynamics in the decision-making process can be very revealing. Humour releases tension as images are rejected. Significant, too, is the way shy members find their voice as they get caught up in the excitement of the exercise. If a cluster struggles to agree on one image, they can choose to describe a composite picture that embraces their different perceptions. In the report back, the reasons given for discarding certain images not only reveal a progression in a cluster's mission thinking, but, even more importantly, how unselfconsciously they began to do theology together.

This exercise can provide a faith-based group with a shared motivation for change, the more so as it is Christologically based. As before, the selected images can be used as a focus for prayer, meditation and worship, giving participants a chance to offer up their hopes and fears to God. The icon of *Christ in Community* affixed to an outer wall of St George's, Tufnell Park, north London, is a prime example of a visual mission statement. Painted by four members of the congregation in 1998, it aimed to give visible expression to their vision of mission – that the Christian faith is found and lived in community. The central figure of Christ symbolizes his compassion and love, while the figures around him reflect all the different shades of life experienced in the Church.

39 – Christ in Community, St George's Tufnell Park

Handout 22
The Pastoral Cycle with Images

The next stage of the exercise involves analysis, theological reflection, prayer and planning for action. This should follow as soon as possible. Once more, images can be used in the Pastoral (Hermeneutical) Cycle popularly known as the *See, Judge, Act* model (see endnote 1). But first, the fellowship must decide on the issue to be tackled, the range of possibilities being daunting.[5] An example of a common issue would be:

'How to develop the life and mission of our faith community?'

See

- Analyze the present situation in your church or fellowship group by choosing an image of Christ, in response to the question:

'Which image of Christ best reflects the present life and mission of our faith community?'

- Meditate on your chosen image for a short period.
- Share your reflections in small groups.
- Feed back your findings to a plenary session of the whole group.

Working with images seems to penetrate even the most indomitable defences to expose the reality of a situation, however uncomfortable that might be. They may well portray an exclusive, inward-looking fellowship more concerned with what takes place inside its confines than outside. The analysis can be sharpened by working through such issues as:

- List the good things, and the not so good things, in your fellowship.
- List those things that need to be affirmed and developed.
- List those things that do not work and need to be discarded.
- What is missing and needs to be introduced?

'What images of Christ would we select to reflect renewed life and mission in our fellowship?'

An analysis of the context in which the fellowship finds itself is also necessary so that an outward-looking focus in mission will relate to the concerns of the community, whatever they might be. Mission audits abound if a more detailed analysis is required.

Judge

- Time is now given to prayer and theological reflection.
- Appropriate biblical themes and passages are chosen for reflection.
- The images of Christ selected above are used as an aid to meditation.
- Discuss any issues that may arise.

Bible study is a common pursuit in British churches, but this seldom leads to any action. However, issues that have surfaced during the *Judge* stage will require a considered response. At the same time, action which feeds into frenetic busy-ness is counter-productive, wasting valuable energy and resources. At this juncture, images can again be used to provide a *Visual Mission Statement for Planning and Action*. These images can be compared with those chosen in the *See* stage in order to clarify the steps that need to be taken to move from 'how we are now' to 'what we want to be and do'. Questions in the planning stage could include:

Act

- How do the images of where we are now relate to the images of where we want to be in the Jesus story?
- In the light of our learning from the Pastoral Cycle, what does God want of us?
- What are the Kingdom issues with which we need to engage?

In planning a strategy for action, both short-term and long-term goals need to be identified, together with a timescale, so ensuring accountability in realizing the goals. The 'who, why, what, where, when, and how' questions are a key component, too, as is the need to sustain interest. One team ministry had their action plan as a regular item on their council agenda so as to monitor progress and keep their churches fully informed. But this is not the end of the process. Confidence gained in achieving even modest goals provides the motivation for a new round of the Pastoral Cycle. Once more, the life and mission of the fellowship is analysed so that further Kingdom issues can be addressed.

40 – Crucifixion scene, South Africa

Handout 23
Bible Study and Talk – Receiving From the World Church: Africa

---

Bible Study 4: Acts 8.26–39

Superficially, this text reads like a vindication of the traditional passage of Christian mission from the First World to the Third. Apostle Philip is seen as bringing the gospel to the Ethiopian eunuch in the desert. However, a closer look shows that it is the humble eunuch who has the more radical insight. Out of all the OT, he picks the Song of the Suffering Servant from Isaiah for his meditation. This points to the image of God in Jesus suffering in solidarity with his creation. In this, the eunuch leads the many believers from the Third World who know how to ask the right questions about the true nature of Jesus, his mission and the Kingdom community he came to establish. From them, the European Church received the good news that justice and liberation are an integral part of Christian salvation. The eunuch's eagerness to seek baptism signalled his commitment to be part of the new Kingdom community. The value of Africa's mission to the rest of the world lies in the probing questions they continue to raise, exposing how we in the West have so often compromised the gospel of Christ.

- What is your understanding of baptism? Is it just a rite of private salvation, or a commitment to be part of the Kingdom community?
- What lesson has the Ethiopian eunuch for us as we go about reading our daily scripture?

Talk: Receiving from the World Church: Africa

Christian mission has suffered a bad press in our time, its past support of Western imperialism and colonialism leaving an enduring legacy of guilt. This has not been helped by the common view of overseas mission as involving charitable giving from the richer West to the suffering poor in some distant land. What is often forgotten is that mission is a reciprocal process. We too must learn to receive. The global centre of Christianity is now in Africa and we can be greatly enriched by the immediacy and vitality of its people's faith, and their unwavering trust in God.

Traditional African spirituality is a lived experience, expressed through words and action – in dancing and singing, ululating and rhythmic percussion, drumming and clapping, extempore prayers and impassioned preaching, processions in church to celebrate important events, baptisms in rivers and in the sea, anointing before a journey, and so on. A normal Sunday service can easily last four hours, followed by feasting. Church members, including children, may well have walked long distances to be present, this being the highlight of their week.

When people in Africa hear the story of Jesus, they experience it as their own story, as if he was being incarnated in their midst. The good news of the crucified and risen Christ revives their faith, giving them hope and courage to face suffering and oppression, and to sustain their struggle for the Kingdom. This was very much the case in South Africa during the apartheid era. As the townships went up in flames, even funeral processions were banned because they provided one of the few opportunities for protest. The sight of Archbishop Desmond Tutu marching ahead with a large wooden cross was a visible witness that the Church had become deeply involved in prophetic action. Not even the army, charged with keeping the increasingly draconian laws, dared to intervene. Through people like him, the cross became a powerful symbol of non-violent resistance in South Africa.

Handout 24
Christ, the Prince of Peace

Story 7: Christ, the Prince of Peace

As regards images of Christ, loyalty to the missionary tradition in Africa died hard, and European images of a white Holy Family continued to be imported from overseas at great expense. In the 1920s, when black Anglican students in the Transvaal began to incorporate African motifs in their wood-carvings, their compatriots complained that a black image of Christ diminished his status. Fortunately, there were others, like Dr Khaketla in Lesotho, who disagreed, saying: 'I don't want a namby-pamby willowy-white Jesus, reclining on his disciples' breast; but a Jesus who is one of us, in our situation, where we are. *This* is the Incarnation.'[6]

In southern Africa, tapestries have been the preferred medium of artwork, focusing on safe biblical themes such as the Madonna and Child, Christ's ministry, and the Last Supper. But as the black consciousness movement gained momentum, the imagery became ever more radical. In Johannesburg, Khotso House – the House of Peace – was formerly the headquarters of the South African Council of Churches and the Anglican Church. The large tapestry that dominated the entrance hall showed a black Christ as the Prince of Peace, standing with arms outstretched to embrace South Africans of every race and in every walk of life, sharing the

41 – Khotso House tapestry, South Africa

struggle of his suffering people for justice and freedom. It was a powerful icon of faith triumphing over evil, and extremely contentious to those in power.

In August 1988, Khotso House was destroyed by a massive bomb planted in the car park below. This was part of the systematic, violent campaign against the Churches. But Church leaders responded by saying 'that the determination by the vast majority of Christians in South Africa to end apartheid and establish God's justice . . . cannot be destroyed'. The wall-hanging remained unscathed above a gaping hole in the floor and the shattered remains of walls and windows. However, it mysteriously disappeared after this incident and has not been seen since. What was most amazing during this time was that, even in the midst of unspeakable horrors, the ethos of African worship remained joyous.

Story 8: What Africans are Doing to Jesus

Among black theologians, there has been a concerted move to integrate African cosmology with their contemporary experience of life. As the South African theologian, Tinyiko Maluleke, so cogently notes: 'Africans are doing a lot of things with Jesus. They are making him sing and dance. They speak through him and he through them.' For Maluleke, Jesus is no longer the high and mighty king, far removed from the world below, nor is he obsessed with judging sinners. Rather, he is a healer without equal, who 'makes people to "be all right"', and enables them to deal with the realities of their lives:

He is a screaming Jesus – screaming on the cross and screaming in Africa, on the pulpits, in the streets and in the squatter camp. The African Christ who smiles on the cross is a paradox inviting reflection. This is a defiant smile. A smile that smiles away the pain of the cross. Africans are taking Jesus by the hand, teaching him a few African 'moves' and sensitizing him to local issues and conditions.[7]

New faces of Christ across the African continent include Ancestor, Elder Brother, Chief, Black Messiah, Healer, Wonder-worker, Story-teller, Protector against Evil Powers, Traditional African Doctor, Master of Initiation, Folk Hero, Liberator, Freedom Fighter, Refugee, Suffering Christ, Sacrifical Offering, Friend of the Poor and the Oppressed, and Christ the Soccer Champion.

Handout 25
An African Liturgy for Mission with African Images of Christ

Images of an African Christ include the 'Vie de Jesus Mafa' set from north Cameroons, and some in 'The Christ We Share' pack. These are placed in the centre of the group, together with a candle and a cross. Images can also be projected from the CD-ROM onto a wall or screen. Start by sitting quietly and reflecting on the images.

Greeting

Leader   Peace be to this house. (Luke 10.5)
All   Not the peace of this world, but the peace of our Lord Jesus Christ. Amen. (John 14.27)

Light the candle.

The Collect for Purity from Kenya

Almighty God, You bring to light things hidden in darkness, and know the shadows of our hearts: cleanse and renew us by your Spirit, that we may walk in the light and glorify your name, through Jesus Christ, the light of the world. Amen.[8]

Celebrating the Saints and Martyrs of Africa

Leader	For Africa, the land of martyrs, prophets and saints,
All	thanks be to God.
Leader	For Simon of Cyrene who carried the cross of Jesus,
All	thanks be to God.
Leader	For Bishops Augustine and Cyprian,
All	thanks be to God.
Leader	For the Martyrs of Uganda,
All	thanks be to God.
Leader	For Bernard Mazeki, martyr of Zimbabwe,
All	thanks be to God.
Leader	For Manche Masemola, virgin and martyr of Sekhukhuneland, South Africa,
All	thanks be to God.
Leader	For Ntsikana, prophet, poet and Xhosa saint,
All	thanks be to God.
Leader	For the healing of the people of Africa,
All	thanks be to God.

Readings

Matthew 28.16–20; Acts 8.26–39.

Meditation: Ntsikana, African prophet, poet and Xhosa saint

Ntsikana (*c.* 1760–1821) is regarded as the first Christian among the Xhosa-speaking people of South Africa. He had a traditional upbringing, being renowned as a singer, dancer and orator. After brief contact with a missionary who headed the white advance into his country, he had a vision in his cattle byre, which he interpreted as a calling from God. He subsequently collected together a small band of disciples who met together twice daily for prayers, praise and instruction in the Word of God.

Although Ntsikana introduced radical new beliefs and practices, he retained continuity with his tradition in composing his Great Hymn, the first in Xhosa. The imagery he uses draws its power from being rooted in the experience of his people: cosmology, leadership, hunting, fighting and the pastoral life. But he uses it in a Christian context. Similarly, the music is based on a Xhosa wedding song; and the literary form is that of a praise poem, like the psalms, but the praise is of God as creator, protector and defender, rather than his chief; and the focus is on Christ. This marked the beginnings of an indigenous African theology, way ahead of its time. In southern Africa, Ntsikana is revered as a prophet and saint, his Great Hymn appearing as No. 1 in most African hymn books.[9]

Ntsikana's Great Hymn

He, is the Great God, who is in heaven.
Thou art thou, true shield, protector.
Thou art thou, true fortress, stronghold.
Thou art thou, true forest of refuge.
Thou art thou, true rock of power.
Thou art thou, who dwells in the highest.
He, who created life (below), created (life) on
    high.
That Creator who created, created the skies.
This maker of stars and the Pleiades.
A star flashed forth, it was telling us.
The maker of the blind, does he not make them
    of purpose?
The trumpet has sounded, it too has called us.
As for His chase, He hunts for souls.
He, who gathers together flocks rejecting each
    other.
He, the leader, who has led us.
He, the Great Blanket, we do put it on.
Those hands of Thine, they are wounded.
Those feet of Thine, they are wounded.
Thy blood, why is it streaming?
Thy blood, it was shed for us.
This great price, have we called for it?
This homestead of Thine, have we called for it?
Little Lamb – you are the Messiah.[10]

*42 – Ntsikana Ongcwele
(Saint Ntsikana),
South Africa*

Archbishop Tutu's Prayer

Goodness is stronger than evil;
Love is stronger than hate;
Light is stronger than darkness;
Life is stronger than death;
Victory is ours through Him who loved us.[11]

Participants share the Peace.

43 – Free at Last,
Archbishop Tutu

Notes

1 Laurie Green, 1990, *Let's Do Theology*, A Pastoral Cycle Resource Book, London: Mowbray, p. 4.

2 Personal communication.

3 Personal communication.

4 Personal communication.

5 For example Steven Croft, 2002, *Transforming Communities: Re-imagining the Church for the 21st Century*, London: Darton, Longman and Todd; and Robert Warren, 2004, *The Healthy Churches' Handbook*, London: Church House Publishing.

6 Interviewed by Janet Hodgson, 1982.

7 T. S. Maluleke, 1997, 'What Africans are doing to Jesus: will he ever be the same again?', in C. W. Du Toit (ed.), *Images of Jesus*, Pretoria: UNISA (University of South Africa), p. 200.

8 A Kenyan Service of Holy Communion, 1990, Nairobi: Uzima Press.

9 Janet Hodgson, 1984, 'The Genius of Ntsikana' in Landeg White and Tim Couzens (eds), *Literature and Society in Southern Africa*, Cape Town: Maskew Miller Longman, pp. 24–40.

10 John Knox Bokwe, 1914, *Ntsikana: The Story of an African Convert*, Lovedale: Lovedale Press, p. 26.

11 Used with permission.

5

THE YOUNG SHALL
SEE VISIONS

44 – Christ entering Jerusalem on a donkey to the jubilation of children[1]

The prophet Joel offers us the grand vision of the coming of the Day of Yahwe at the end of times when all God's people fulfil their potential. He enthuses about the young men and women being able to witness things which were not visible in ordinary times. This chapter, which trains young people's powers of perception of Christ's mission, takes its title from the prophecy of Joel: 'Your young people shall see visions' (cf. Joel 28.2).

Introductory Talk: No More Mr Nice Guy

All-age workshops have enabled people across three generations to come together to share their faith and stretch their imaginations. The insights of young people continue to amaze and to challenge. Three girls in a parish group chose No More Mr Nice Guy as their image of Christ, a cover illustration of a Student Christian Movement magazine in 1994. A laid-back-looking Christ is depicted with orange hair, a green crown of thorns and a glowing cigarette between his lips. As the editorial explained:

> The sugar-coated Jesus has to go. The image of Jesus as universal Mr Nice Guy is as familiar and comforting as a shabby teddy bear and as much use. *No More Mr Nice Guy* invites us to think again about Jesus, to shed our sentimental imagery in favour of a Jesus who has direct relevance to our age, who speaks to our concerns and who bites.

While adults found the picture offensive, the girls felt that such an image would provoke their non-Christian school-friends to at least begin asking questions about this man Jesus and to be sufficiently intrigued to want to discover more. They argued that their peers were far more likely to relate to this picture than the images normally found in churches, and that the editorial was spot on.

45 – No more
Mr Nice Guy

Handout 26
Workshop Material for 'The Young Shall See Visions'

Various workshops from Handout 26 can be selected according to the requirements of the group, their ages and abilities, the nature of the event and the time available. Visual images of Christ provide a basic resource covering a wide range of interests. They can be used in classroom activities in Religious Studies and Art and in working with youth groups, Sunday schools, children's groups, all-age gatherings, those preparing for confirmation, fresh expressions groups, etc.

Refreshments are provided as required.

The Young Shall See Visions

5 minutes:	Introductory Talk: 'No More Mr Nice Guy'.
Variable:	*Handout 27: Art Projects with images of Christ.*
	Handout 28: Exercises with images of Christ.
c. 1 hour:	Exercise 12: 'Using Images Together with Jesus' "I AM" Sayings'.
c. 1 hour:	Exercise 13: 'Exploring Gospel Themes Using Images'.
30 minutes:	Exercise 14: 'How Do We Imitate Jesus to be Worthy Disciples?'
Variable:	*Handout 29: Images of Christ in Sacred Spaces.*
c. 1 hour:	*Handout 30: The Faith We See.*
	Story 9: 'Seeing is Better than Hearing'.
	Story 10: '"Your sons and daughters shall prophesy"'.
	Handout 31: Bible studies.
c. 1 hour:	Bible study 5: Luke 2.41–52.
c. 1 hour:	Bible study 6: John 6.41–2.
Variable:	*Handout 32: Youth Mission Prayer (Christian Conference of Asia).*
Variable:	*Handout 33: Affirmation of Faith (Botswana).*
Variable:	*Handout 34: Silent Meditation (England).*
Variable:	*Handout 35: Young People's Worship Service.*

Handout 27
Art Projects with Images of Christ

Project 1

In Bearpark, a former pit village in County Durham, a class of pre-primary schoolchildren worked with a selected range of images. These included Christmas cards because of the likely familiarity of the Nativity as a gospel story. After a brief explanation, the children chose the pictures they wished to draw. These were later compiled by their teacher into a book, with their comments, and given to me as a gift. Most of the children had only minimal knowledge of Christianity, if any, but their enthusiasm was infectious. A lively discussion during the process kept us on our toes.

46 – Face of Jesus, Madonna and Child, Jesus with Children

Project 2

During a time of racial tension in a multiracial school in South London, I worked alongside a gifted art teacher with a class of teenagers. Each student was asked to choose an image of Christ and then make his or her own interpretation of the pictures in different media – paint, crayon, charcoal and clay. Some students were from different faith backgrounds, others from none. Most had little or no knowledge of Christianity. In the subsequent discussion, they asked penetrating questions about who this Christ was and why he had been depicted so differently in diverse cultures. They then reflected on their own artwork and what they themselves had tried to achieve. The visual impact of the images succeeded where words would have made little impact.

Project 3

Both Lat Blaylock and Margaret Cooling provide a host of resources and activities for linking religious education with art for different age groups in schools. For example, in his Pack B (2004), Blaylock draws on the work of 16 contemporary artists worldwide to tell the story of Jesus from the manger to the cross – and beyond. Each large picture card is backed with biblical extracts, provocative questions and information about the artwork. A 24-page guide to classroom use across the 7–18 age range is included. This gives a detailed description of the teaching and learning approaches followed, offering flexible and creative ideas in presenting the Gospel stories. There is added value in seeing how global Christian communities express their faith in Jesus through the arts. Learners are encouraged to engage with the material in a critical manner, expressing their own insights into Jesus and into the issues which concerned him.[2]

Margaret Cooling's work on *Jesus through Art* is an equally creative resource for teaching RE through art. Large colour prints, spiral-bound for whole-group use, are combined with extensive notes and teaching material. Unfortunately, some of her publications are presently out of print and would need to be accessed through an RE resource centre or library.[3]

Project 4

Drawings of various symbols associated with Christ – such as a peacock, pelican, lamb, cross, a bunch of grapes, a sheaf of wheat, anchor, fish, pilgrim shell, keys, etc. – can be printed on a sheet of paper and used as a handout for schoolchildren visiting a church so as to familiarize them with Christian imagery. As a fun exercise they are asked to look for the various symbols as they go round the building and tick them off.

Similarly, a coloured photocopy of works of art in the church, such as stained-glass windows, paintings, icons, statues, kneelers, banners, crosses and crucifixes, altar frontals and carvings on pulpit, font and screen, is used as a handout in the same way. Once the tasks are done, the leader or minister can give a short talk on the age-old role of Christian images in teaching people about the Christian faith.[4]

Project 5

Children can be told a Gospel story and then asked to draw a picture relating to it. Such images of Christ could include:

- Working with his father in a carpenter's shop.
- The Good Shepherd tending his sheep.
- Giving out the law on the mountain top.
- Raising Lazarus and the centurion's daughter from the dead.
- Healing the blind, the sick and the disabled, such as the paralysed man let down through the roof by his friends.
- The miracle worker feeding the five thousand.
- The angry revolutionary in the Temple.
- The host cooking a breakfast of fish for his disciples by the lakeside.
- Riding on a donkey into Jerusalem.
- The party giver at the wedding at Cana.
- The long-distance walker with his followers (e.g. from the Sea of Galilee to Jerusalem and on the road to Emmaus).
- Praying in the Garden of Gethsemane.
- Carrying the cross to Calvary.

Another exercise would be to ask children to get into the mind of Jesus and write a letter to him asking what it *felt like*:

- to be riding on a donkey to Jerusalem surrounded by an excited crowd of children waving palm branches;
- to spend 40 days in the wilderness and be tempted by the devil;
- to be tossed around in a stormy sea with his terrified disciples;
- to walk on water;
- to overturn the tables of the moneylenders in the Temple;
- to cook fish on the lake shore for his hungry disciples;
- to bless and share bread and wine at the Last Supper, etc.

These letters could be accompanied by drawings or paintings and, if appropriate, used in a church magazine or put on display.

A third task would be to ask children to invent modern images of Jesus and illustrate them – with paint, crayons, clay, charcoal, plasticine and the like. Such images could include Jesus as an asylum-seeker, homeless wanderer, refugee, beggar, non-violent protestor, inner-city youth, rape victim, apprentice tradesman, etc. A discussion could then follow as to why each artist chose a particular image.

Handout 28
Exercises with Images of Christ

JESUS SAID J AM THE WAY
THE TRUTH+THE LJFE

47 – Jesus said, 'I am the Way, the Truth and the Life'.

Exercise 12: Using Images together with Jesus' 'I AM' sayings

Jesus made several statements which begin with 'I am . . .' Look up references
in John's Gospel and complete the sentences. Jesus said:

- I am .... (John 6.35)
- I am .... (John 8.12)
- I am .... (John 10.7)
- I am .... (John 10.11)
- I am .... (John 11.25)
- I am .... (John 14.6)
- I am .... (John 15.1)
- Draw pictures of the some of the 'I am . . .' sayings.
- Discuss the role of symbols as images of Jesus in the sayings.
- Try to find images of the sayings in other cultures. What differences can
  you see from images in your own culture?

Answers to the 'I am . . .' sayings in Endnote 5.

48 – 'I AM' symbols

Exercise 13: Exploring Gospel Themes Using Images

Working in pairs, find images from other cultures of different Gospel themes. Compare them with images in your own culture.

- For example, the Nativity, baptism of Christ, Christ in the wilderness, events leading up to the crucifixion, resurrection appearances, ascension.
- Christ's ministry of healing, teaching, celebrating.
- The parables.
- Christ calling and sending disciples.
- Christ with different people – his parents, Mary and Martha, Peter, Zacchaeus, rich young man, children, the woman at the well, Mary Magdalene, Nicodemus, disciples as fishermen, wedding at Cana.

Still working in pairs, find gospel passages to match the images for your chosen theme. Discuss your findings as a group.

What are your new insights as to how people around the world see Jesus?

Exercise 14: How Do We Imitate Jesus to be Worthy Disciples?

What does it mean to be sent out as a disciple of Christ? What would be expected of me? Decide on three aspects as listed below:

- A friend to others, no matter who they are.
- Available when needed.
- Compassionate and caring.
- Never afraid to speak one's mind and be prophetic.
- Prepared to take risks whatever the cost.
- Forgiving others who have wronged me.
- Accepting people just as they are.
- Working alongside the poor and the powerless.
- Prepared to fight for justice and truth.
- Any other aspects of your own choosing?

Can you find any images which correspond with your chosen aspects? Explain your chosen aspects to a partner.

Handout 29
Images of Christ in Sacred Spaces

Janet Marshall spent 15 years in sacred space education while working at the Shrine of Our Lady at Walsingham, Norfolk, offering learning experiences for all ages in an alternative educational (sacred space) setting.

According to her, the Shrine contains a fascinating collection of visual images such as statues, wall paintings, icons, stained-glass windows, Stations of the Cross, etc., and she soon became aware that children and young people responded well to such imagery. In order to stimulate their thinking and to prepare them for responding visually, emotionally and spiritually to images within the Shrine and gardens, it was necessary to prepare them for this experience. She therefore began to collect sets of images, ranging from the contemporary to the traditional, of Christ, Mary and the saints from around the world, as well as crosses and crucifixes. The young people would be asked to sort images into groups and then discuss their response to them. They would then think about how such things might help Christians to pray and worship. This proved to be an excellent preparation for their Shrine experience.

The youngsters would also be asked to create their own images through artwork, or produce visual prayers using images rather than words. They might even write poetry based on what they had seen, often while spending silent times looking around the Shrine. This was a great help to teachers in achieving what they could not do in their RE lessons at school, provoking lively discussion about faith and practice.

49 – The Presentation

Images and sacred objects were also used in creative prayer sessions as part of youth events. All of this was said to have played a significant part in the spiritual development of children and young people.[6]

Handout 30
The Faith We See

Story 9: Seeing is Better than Hearing

A true story from South Africa shows how seeing rather than hearing makes for better evangelism. John was a brilliant student, but his unkempt, shabby appearance was rather off-putting to his elders. The well-dressed, middle-class, conservative church opposite the campus decided to launch a ministry to students but were somewhat taken aback when John walked in one Sunday, with his tattered jeans, wild hair and bare feet. The church was packed, with not a seat to spare. The congregation held its breath as John, undeterred, walked to the front and squatted on the carpet, as would have happened in any student fellowship.

The service was just about to start and tension rose as an elderly, silver-haired deacon, with pocket watch and three-piece suit, slowly made his way to the front. He walked with a cane, and as he started making his way toward the boy, the congregation was thinking, 'How can you expect a man of his age and background to understand some college kid sitting on the floor?' It took a long time for the deacon to reach the boy. Except for the clicking of his cane, there was dead silence as the people held their breath, waiting for the expected showdown. To their utter amazement, when the deacon finally reached John, he dropped his cane and, with great difficulty, lowered himself painfully to the floor, sitting down next to John, so he would not be alone. Everyone was choked with emotion. When the minister, waiting patiently in the pulpit, finally gained control, he said, 'What I'm about to preach, you will never remember. What you have just seen, you will never forget.'[7]

The minister was right. Seeing is a far better tool for religious teaching than hearing a lot of sermons and talks, which are soon forgotten. Once we see an image, it sticks in our memory and can have a profound influence on our life, as has been proven time and again in working with images of Christ. In a world of computer games and television, visual aids such as sacred images are a far more effective instrument for Christian education than a deluge of words.

• Would you prefer ministers to use imagery in their sermons and teaching rather than too many words? If so, why?

50 – Crucifixion

Story 10: 'Your sons and daughters shall prophesy' (Joel 2.28)

In the mid-1990s, the youth group at St John the Evangelist Church in Birtley, north-east England, had to decide how best to invest their precious savings of £80. In an adaptation of the Pastoral Cycle (see Chapter 3), they used images of Christ to seek justice and truth from the local banking industry. Led by Brenda Jones, an experienced Mission Enabler (now a priest), the youngsters, aged between 13 and 17, worked with two images in order to formulate ethical criteria in selecting a bank.

First, they held a brainstorming session to reflect on how they saw Jesus at the present time. They then divided into two groups. One group was given the image of *The Laughing Christ* (*The Christ We Share*, no. 1), created by the Canadian artist, Willis S. Wheatley, in 1973.[8] The other group received the image of *The Angry Christ* (*The Christ We Share*, no. 9) from the Philippines. This was painted by Lino Pantebon from the Negros Islands in 1975 and depicts a furious Christ with the long hair and beard of a sugar plantation worker. He points an accusing finger at the local sugar barons, who exploit their workers through starvation wages and oppressive feudal conditions. But it is an image which transcends cultural constraints, finding common cause with exploited people everywhere. Using these two images, the youngsters were asked to discuss:

- What do you like or dislike about the image?
- What surprises you about it?
- What does your image communicate to you about Christ?
- How does your image compare with your original depiction of Jesus?

Those working with *The Laughing Christ* felt that God does not will suffering, and that even in the midst of oppression there can be joy. Quoting the Beatitudes in Luke's Gospel (6.21), that 'those who weep today will laugh tomorrow', they thought that change was already taking place; but wondered how the powerful, who expect the poor to weep, would account for their laughter. In their thinking they quite unknowingly came close to the artist's original concept of his image as *Jesus Christ, Liberator.*

The other group had no problem equating the anger of Christ with an unfair, unequal world and with the way people's lives are manipulated by forces outside their control. They could easily identify with this experience themselves. Reflecting on these insights, the entire group was then asked what questions they would like to ask a number of banks before opening an account. They came up with the following:

- What is the policy of your bank on reducing Third World debt?
- Does your bank loan money to organizations involved in selling arms?
- How does your bank support the care of the environment?

The same letter was sent to all the banks in town, but only one took it seriously. This bank manager admitted ignorance and the need to consult a senior colleague. A formal reply was eventually sent, answering all the youngsters' queries. This process enabled them to become involved in ongoing discussions and to realize that, in some small way, they had the power to challenge the *status quo*. For those who feel overwhelmed by powerlessness, this was a major step forward. Other banks either did not bother to reply or else sent a standard pack of glossy information as to how to open an account. Not surprisingly, the Birtley youth group opted for the first bank and reported back to the parish their reasons for doing so.

The facilitator for such a process needs to provide:

- information about the images used;
- leading questions to draw out discussion;
- Bibles for theological reflection, with suitable references;
- time for meditation and prayer;
- help with planning for any action that might arise from a discussion.

51 – Christ in the Temple

Handout 31
Bible Studies

Bible Study 5: Luke 2.41–52

The boy Jesus runs away to spend time with the elders of the community. His parents did not understand his behaviour and naturally scold him. Jesus politely tells them about his desire to be about his Father's business. He uses his free will to explore his vocation yet the Scripture tells us that he remained obedient to his parents. By keeping a balance between his free spirit and parental obedience, he pleased both God and his family.

- How important is it to you to explore your spiritual goals and purpose in life while still young? Share in a group discussion.
- Discuss the challenge of reconciling free spirit with obedience to elders in the family.
- Are your family relationships a hindrance or a help in your growth as a person? Discuss positive and negative aspects.

Bible Study 6: John 6.41–42

In spite of his extraordinary gifts and abilities, Jesus lived as a normal person under his parents' roof, plying his apprenticeship as a carpenter. Preparing himself for his ministry, he went about his business without fanfare. People knew him as an ordinary resident of Galilee and as the son of Mary and Joseph, a sign of how much the young Jesus was part of the family and the community and not a rebellious outsider.

- How would Jesus have responded to some of the challenges faced by modern youth, such as the consumer and celebrity cultures, lack of role models, sexual promiscuity, drugs, benefit culture?
- Share with the group what you think a normal working day would have looked like in the early life of Jesus.
- Jesus had several siblings. Imagine you are one of them. Write a letter to Jesus imagining that he was an older brother or sister.

Handout 32
Youth Mission Prayer (Christian Conference of Asia)

Leader	Lord, give us churches that will not merely comfort the afflicted,
All	but afflict the comfortable;
Leader	churches that will not only love the world,
All	but will judge the world;
Leader	churches that will not only pursue peace,
All	but will also demand justice;
Leader	churches that will not pass by on the other side,
All	when wounded humanity is waiting to be healed;
Leader	churches that not only call us to worship,
All	but also send us out to witness;
Leader	churches who will follow Christ,
All	even when the way points to the cross. Amen.[9]

52 – Christ and the children

Handout 33
Affirmation of Faith (Botswana)

Used by Canon Ronald Wynne in his ministry to the Mbukushu people, refugees from Angola, who settled in north-western Botswana in 1967.

The people repeat each clause after the leader with appropriate gestures.

We believe (*arms raised above the head with feet apart*);
that God sent his Son Jesus into the world (*hands brought down close together and stretched in front of the body*);
he became man through the Holy Spirit (*hands cross to resemble the wings of a dove*);
he was born of the Virgin Mary (*hands clasped in a mime of cradling by a mother, with head turned and eyes cast down*);
he was crucified (*arms stretched out*);
died (*head dropped forward*);
and was buried (*head lying on the arm, as though in sleep*);
he went down to those below (*fingers touching the ground*);
afterwards he rose from the dead (*arms raised, stretched out in front of the body, parallel to the ground, with palms upturned*);
and he went up into heaven to sit at God's right hand (*hands raised above the head*);
there he prays for us always (*palms of hands joined together above the head*);
Praise the Lord (*hands outspread above the head*).[10]

Handout 34
Silent Meditation (England)

The purpose of this short, silent meditation is for young people to learn how important it is to take time off and reflect on things in their personal life and in the life of the wider community under the Lordship of Jesus Christ. After each 'Maranatha' response (meaning 'Come, Lord Jesus'), there is a short silent pause for reflection, gratitude, praise, penitence and resolve for Christian service and action. The duration of the silent pause may vary, depending upon the discretion of the Leader. Images of Christ from the CD-ROM can be projected onto a wall or screen.

Leader   Jesus came to love all beings.
All   Maranatha. Come, Lord Jesus. (*pause*)

Leader	Jesus came to serve all beings.
All	Maranatha. Come, Lord Jesus. (*pause*)
Leader	Jesus came to feed all beings.
All	Maranatha. Come, Lord Jesus. (*pause*)
Leader	Jesus came to free all beings.
All	Maranatha. Come, Lord Jesus. (*pause*)
Leader	Jesus came to bless all beings.
All	Maranatha. Come, Lord Jesus. (*pause*)
Leader	Hallelujah. Lord Jesus is here.
All	He is among us, indeed. Amen.

The meditation can end with the singing of 'Maranatha' from the Iona Community, Scotland.[11]

53 – Jesus goes fishing

Handout 35
A Young People's Worship Service

Selected images from the CD-ROM are projected onto a wall or screen during the service.

Leader	Leap with joy for the grace of our Lord God,
All	and dance with thanks for the love of Jesus Christ.
Leader	Jesus showed us how to love people,
All	and how to treat them with respect.
Leader	Hurray to the Holy Spirit, the giver of life,
All	the giver of youth and strength.

Leader	Let us thank God for giving us so much,
All	and think of those who have so little.

Hymn

'Make me a channel of your peace' (Prayer of St Francis).

Confession (divide into two groups)

Group 1	We have always had so much,
Group 2	but we cared to share so little.
Group 1	We laughed at the weak and old,
Group 2	and ignored the poor and needy.
Group 1	We took so much from others,
Group 2	but we gave back so little to the world.

Absolution

Leader	The Lord God who can search our hearts has heard our confession and grants us forgiveness and strength to make our lives shine.
All	Amen.

Prayer

Lord Jesus, even though you were divine, you chose, as a teenager, to be part of your family and train as a carpenter and earn a living like everybody else; help us to become creative and productive members of our communities. Grant us imagination and boldness to select a vocation, so that by pursuing it diligently we may live to serve you and your people. Amen.

Leader	Let us thank God for our communities,
All	where we may build the Kingdom of God.
Leader	We respect the elderly in the neighbourhood,
All	that they may understand and guide us.
Leader	Give us, Lord, strength to defend the weak,
All	and to help those who are in need.
Leader	Jesus, make us proud Christians,
All	and humble citizens of the whole world.

Blessing

Leader   May God the Father fill us with joy.

May God the Son fill us with love.

May God the Holy Spirit fill us with hope.

And may the blessings of our all-loving God bring us everlasting peace.

All   Amen.

All share the Peace at the end of the service.

Notes

1 The original fresco is in an ancient Coptic church dug out of rock in Lalibela, in the Ethiopian mountains, dating from the thirteenth century. Ethiopia became a Christian kingdom in AD 333, the earliest in Africa, and developed a unique style of art, religious practices and worship. In the fresco, Jesus is holding a palm branch in one hand, while believers pour libations, or drink-offerings, in his path to honour him and the children wave palm branches in jubilation. (cf. John 12.12–16)

2 Lat Blaylock, *Picturing Jesus: Worldwide Contemporary Artists – Pack A* (2001) and *Pack B* (2004), Birmingham: RE Today Services.

3 Margaret Cooling, Jane Taylor and Diane Walker, 1998, *Jesus Through Art: A Resource for Teaching Religious Education and Art*, Norwich: RMEP and 2009, *Christianity Through Art*, Norwich: RMEP.

4 I am indebted to Geoff Lowson, Vicar of Holy Saviour Church, Tynemouth Priory, Newcastle, for this idea.

5 Answers to Jesus' 'I am . . .' sayings: the bread of life; the light of the world; the door of the sheep; the good shepherd; the resurrection; the way, the truth, the life; the true vine.

6 Personal communication. Janet Marshall developed the Education Department at Walsingham between 1995 and 2010 and was part of the Sacred Space Working Group. In her new role as Head of Schools and Families at St Paul's Cathedral, London, she is developing a visit for schools based on Christianity in Art.

7 Vivien Harris (former executive secretary of the Methodist Church in Southern Africa), 1998, 'Actions speak louder than words', *Challenge* 51, Dec. 1998/Jan. 1999, p. 11.

8 When Willis died, the United Church of Canada acquired rights to the original picture, *Jesus Christ, Liberator*. They then allowed Paulist priests in San Francisco to produce it, entitled *The Laughing Christ*.

9 Taken from *Your Will Be Done*, published by CCA Youth, Christian Conference of Asia, n. d. (original source unknown).

10 Ronald Wynne, 1988, *The Pool That Never Dries Up*, London: USPG, p. 84.

11 'Maranatha' in John Bell and Graham Maule, *The Courage to Say No. Twenty-three Songs for Lent and Easter*, Glasgow: Wild Goose Publications, pp. 46–7. Also on tape and CD – good for a singalong. Lat Blaylock has an insert in his *Pack B* (2004) on 'Meditation with Children'.

6

MEDITATING WITH IMAGES

54 – Praying hands

Handout 36
Introduction: Communing with God

Christian prayer is the way to commune with God the Father through his incarnate Son Jesus Christ in the unity of the Holy Spirit. Both the Father and the Holy Spirit are hard to fathom for the finite mind of a believer. It is a sign of God's grace, compassion, wisdom and justice that we have all been given access to God's infinite glory through the mediation of Jesus, who has embraced our humanity. Jesus is thus the image of God on which we focus in prayer.

We pray mostly using words, our own or those prepared by others, to suit our needs. Our prayers can also be in the form of a scriptural sentence, psalmody, praise, hymn, song, chant, mantra, or holy utterance such as 'Maranatha', etc. Some may speak in tongues. Others may prefer the Jesus prayer: 'Jesus Christ, Son of Mary, have mercy on me, a sinner', or merely, 'Lord Jesus, have mercy'. Our prayers may be spoken out loud or in silence. We may pray alone or in a fellowship. Whether said in church, at home, or in the open, our prayers are acceptable to our gracious God.

To support our words we may use candles, votive lights, incense and bells, or assume certain postures such as folded hands, kneeling, sitting, clapping, swaying in a dance, raising our hands and the like. We may also regulate breath to help spoken prayer. Christians have employed this discursive way of praying down the centuries. Often, as in the Celtic, Orthodox, Roman Catholic and Anglican traditions, we pray to the saints, including Mary, asking them to intercede on our behalf with God. Then there are prayers of confession, thanksgiving, intercession, petition and so forth. In all these we use words to link us with God.

There is another traditional mode of prayer which the Church has always used with great benefit. It is the prayer with images, be they images of Jesus, saints, martyrs, Old Testament figures or angels. Our limited human minds find it helpful to focus on finite images pointing to the infinite. The image serves as a gateway to the divine that transcends words and thoughts. In God's presence we are so often struck dumb and become lost for words. This is why images, which require neither words nor thought, help all sorts and conditions of people, from the scholarly to the childlike. What we read or hear is often quickly forgotten, but we seldom forget something we have seen.

As we focus on a sacred image, there is no nagging compulsion to use words, or even to think or rationalize. We just sit and absorb what we see, not only with our eyes but also with our souls. Soon, the image takes on a life of its own and starts working within us, feeding our mind with insights and visions. An added benefit in meditating with an image is that we are free to use words if we so wish. At an advanced stage in meditation, one may eventually let go of the image altogether so as to journey more deeply inwards into the inexhaustible mystery of God, the Father of our Lord Jesus Christ.

Handout 37
Programme for Meditating with Images

Various workshops from Handout 37 can be selected according to the requirements of those involved, the nature of the occasion (private devotions, corporate worship, a course, quiet day, retreat) and the time available.

Refreshments are provided as required.

Programme for Meditating with Images

15 minutes:	*Handout 36: Introduction: Communing with God.*
	Handout 37: Programme for Meditating with Images.
30 minutes:	*Handout 38: Bible study 7: Genesis 1.27, 'God created man in his own image'.*
30 minutes:	*Handout 39: Silent Meditation and Image Meditation.*
Variable:	*Handout 40: Image Meditation Workshop.*
	Image Meditation 1: Jesus Riding a Donkey.
	Image Meditation 2: Agony in the Garden.
	Image Meditation 3: Using the Cross as an Image
15 minutes:	*Handout 41: Aids to Prayer and Meditation.*
30 minutes:	*Handout 42: Bible study 8: Luke 10.38–42.*
Variable:	*Handout 43: Stories and Prayers with Images.*
	Story 11: 'Dürer's *Praying Hands* – Mother Teresa's Prayer'.
	Story 12: 'The Prayer-Life of an Inuit Seal-Hunter – The Prayer of St John of the Cross'.
	Story 13: 'A Latter-Day St Martin – The *Anima Christi*'.
	Story 14: 'The Carne Cross – A Celtic Prayer for Protection: *Encompassing*'.
20 minutes:	*Handout 44: A Deeper Experience of God.*
Variable:	*Handout 45: A Meditative Liturgy.*

Handout 38

Bible Study 7: Genesis 1.27 'God created man in his own image'

Before we learn to pray or meditate, we must first ask ourselves: 'Who is the one who is praying or meditating?' You might reply: 'Of course, I pray.' But the basic question is: 'Who is this "I"?' The Bible's simple answer is that the 'I' who prays or meditates is the very core of our identity: the image of God. We are created in his image. Unless we have this self-understanding, we cannot focus on God. Our self-image is the true engine of all prayer and meditation and the best image with which to start. Otherwise, we shall not benefit from any external images of God and Jesus.

• Who am I in Christ? What do I feel or think about myself?

This question challenges me to look into myself. The enquiry into the nature of Christ is inextricably linked with the enquiry into one's own self-understanding and self-esteem.

• Who is Christ in me? What difference does he make in my life?

We cannot possibly relate to God unless we have come to terms with our own spiritual destiny. Every individual has a unique relationship with God, allowing us to relate to him in many different ways. The more we fulfil our own destiny, the more we are at one with God.

Handout 39
Silent Meditation and Image Meditation

Thanks to the Western Church's exposure to Eastern meditation, silence and meditation are increasingly taking their fair share in the prayer life of believers. Some advocate a study of Eastern religions; others prefer to go back to our lost Christian tradition of meditation as among the early Celts, the Church Fathers and the Orthodoxy. Silent meditation includes:

- getting away from the din and bustle: withdrawing from the world;
- observing total silence;
- relaxing the mind and body, with closed eyes and an upright posture;
- watching the movement of breath;
- preferably being alone; but there should be no social interaction if in fellowship;
- excluding all worldly thoughts and distractions, the goal being to stop the chattering mind and enhance concentration;
- focusing inwardly on one particular sacred theme;
- achieving a still mind, inner peace, tranquillity, clarity, joyfulness;
- opening oneself to the deeper objective of listening to the still, small voice of God;
- possibly using aids such as music, mantras, candles, incense, etc.

55 – Sri Lankan Christ sitting in the lotus position

The Bible enjoins us to 'Be still and know that I am God!' (Psalm 46.10). According to Mark Dyer, Episcopalian American Bishop, 'Silence is the language of God. Everything else is a bad translation.'[1] In the stillness of a silent meditation, we would hope to hear 'God's voice in our lives and the will of God working in the world'.[2] While Archbishop Tutu obviously has in mind God's will in our struggle for justice, more often than not silent meditation tends to blunt our sensitivity to all that is happening in the outside world and tempts us to burrow ever deeper into the comfortable duvets of our private lives.

Thomas Merton, the Trappist monk, popularized what is known as contemplative prayer. As a kind of fusion of Eastern and Western spirituality, it is meditative in the Eastern sense, but retains the Judaeo-Christian element of a personal relationship with God. But it has limitations in that only a few gifted people are able to enter into deep contemplation. This is where an image prayer is so effective in meditation. Accessible to one and all, it has some distinctive benchmarks. These include:

- not emptying the mind of all thoughts, but keeping it alert to the outside world of which the image is a part;
- keeping the eyes open so as to observe the image in all its many dimensions and colours;
- adopting a comfortable but steady posture;
- focusing on the image so as to enter into the world of Jesus;
- becoming part of Jesus' story as depicted in an image;
- doing a Bible study so as to understand the story better;
- transferring the dynamics of the story to the reality of daily life;
- inviting the Lord Jesus into your journey of faith;
- asking yourself what action you feel called upon to heal your life and the life of the wider community;
- praising and thanking Jesus for his ongoing presence and praying for guidance in your journey;
- making use of aids such as music, candles, mantras, incense.

Clearly, an image meditation pulls you back into God's creation instead of taking you away from it. It sharpens all your senses instead of dulling them into an unworldly calmness. It obliges you to engage with the Gospels as though Jesus was with you here and now. Like a time machine, the image helps you recover the world of the historical Jesus and then moves you forward to your calling as a disciple, reshaping your life according to the teaching of Jesus as the living Lord. Last, an image becomes a catalyst for action that may transform life around you.

Archbishop Tutu encourages us to follow Jesus' example in which disengagement, waiting on God, precedes engagement. For Tutu, an authentic spirituality requires that we first spend time with Jesus in the wilderness, seeking the vision of God, before we can take something of this vision back into the world and start dealing with issues such as justice, peace and reconciliation. And then, we must needs take the suffering of our wounded world back to God in prayer and contemplation.[3]

- In discursive prayer, we talk to God.
- In silent prayer, we listen to God.
- In image prayer, we walk with God.

Handout 40
Image Meditation Workshop

An image meditation involves engaged prayer, a close study of the Scripture behind the image, an observant focus on the image itself, a lively imagination, much soul-searching, a firm resolve to personalize the image in one's own faith life and, last but not least, a steady posture. Below are three practical demonstrations of how to do it.

Image Meditation 1: Jesus Riding a Donkey into Jerusalem

Read carefully the different accounts of the incident in all four Gospels: Matthew 21.4–12; Mark 11.7–11; Luke 19.35–45; John 2.13–16, 12.12–15. Compare them before you focus on the image.

56 – Entry into Jerusalem

Become one of the citizens cheering Jesus on, singing 'Hosanna', waving palm fronds, clapping and celebrating. Where are you in the scene? Who are you? Are you a child, an adult, one of the apostles, or the man laying down the carpet? Are you even the donkey on which Jesus rode? What is your response? What do you feel?

Describe your emotions about the cleansing of the Temple. Put yourself in the shoes of one of the Pharisees or a Roman guard. What does this scene remind you of in any present situation in your world today? How differently would you respond to the situation after having been through the Jerusalem scene with Jesus? What would you do? Why?

Image Meditation 2: Agony in the Garden of Gethsemane – Luke 22.39–46

Observe the image prayerfully in conjunction with a careful reading of the passage. Picture the events unfolding in the garden. Jesus is alone, full of fear and on the brink of being tested. Where are you in the scene? Are you by his side praying with him, or just looking on? Or are you one of the sleeping disciples? Do you sense Jesus' pain and loneliness? He is sweating drops of blood. Can you put yourself in his place? We can never compare our pain with his, but have you ever found yourself in a traumatic situation like this? Tell Jesus how you felt.

57 – The Agony in the Garden

Jesus is feeling a sense of betrayal, too. While he prayed, his disciples slept close by. Do you remember those occasions when you betrayed the trust of someone dear to you? Recall times when you disappointed God by letting others down through cowardice or apathy. Spiritually speaking, do you feel remorseful about your faith life? Is this image encouraging you to be more on your guard? Where do you seek solace when you become sorry about your lack of commitment? In Jesus, of course, but where else? Do you have any spiritual companions to support you? In the garden, Jesus is being comforted by angels. Where are your angels? Thank them for divine intervention. Conclude the meditation with a short prayer of confession and seek absolution from the praying Jesus in the image.

Image Meditation 3: Using the Cross as an Image

Canon Morriat Ncela Gabula, from Lusikisiki in South Africa, sent us a moving account of a workshop he once led for the Mothers' Union in his parish. They had come together to make palm crosses for the Passion Sunday service. One woman felt that, as she plaited the palm fronds, it was as if a cross was being plaited inside of her and that she was, in a way, reliving the whole drama of the Passion of her Lord. This is a classic example of how an external image can become an inner experience in the heart of a believer. Through prayer, the other women also seem to have transported themselves into the presence of the crucified Lord. They became very emotional as this experience spoke directly to their personal situations. However, at the end, there was also much rejoicing at the realization of how close Jesus was to them in their suffering. They went home elated and empowered.

Before meditating on the cross as an image, read the Passion narrative in at least one Gospel. (If you regularly use the cross as an image, then read and compare the accounts in all four Gospels.) Study your chosen narrative carefully. If you are focusing on a painting of the crucifixion, try to rediscover the narrative as portrayed in the painting. Imagine that you are actually present at Golgotha with John and the three Marys. Relive the event in every detail. Relate it to a situation in which you are experiencing struggle, fear or stress. Sense how Jesus is in solidarity with you and others around you. Experience the cross of Jesus as the source of healing and comfort. Conclude with a prayer of thanksgiving and ask for courage to endure your cross, whatever that might be.[4]

58 – Sixth Station of the Cross, Jesus meets his Mother

Handout 41
Aids to Prayer and Meditation

A Holding Cross

A wooden holding cross is a more tactile and three-dimensional aid to meditation and prayer. Made from different woods, the holding cross has an uneven transverse beam so as to fit comfortably between the fingers while being cradled in the palm of the hand. Angela Ashwin has provided a leaflet with appropriate prayers. But a holding cross is also a symbolic image of Christ and it can become an encounter with the living Jesus himself. Holding the cross in silence is in itself a meditation or prayer. As Ashwin explains: 'Maybe you have no words anyway and it is through your sense of touch that you are expressing your love of Christ and your need of him.'[5] One of her prayers is as follows:

59 – A holding cross

O Lord, Jesus Christ,
stay beside me to defend me,
within me to guide me,
before me to lead me,
behind me to guard me,
and above me to bless me;
that with you and in you
I may live and move and have my being,
for ever and ever. (Source unknown)

Prayer Beads

Since early times, people have used pebbles, a string of knots or beads, or some form of rosary, as a focus for meditative prayer. Anglican prayer beads are a relatively new form, using a blend of the Roman Catholic rosary and the Orthodox Jesus prayer rope. In contrast to the Catholic rosary, which is used to pray to the Virgin Mary and focus on the seminal events in the life of Christ, the prayer beads are mainly used as a tactile aid to contemplative or meditative prayer. It is customary

60 – Prayer beads

to start with the symbolic imagery of the cross and the saying of the Lord's Prayer. Anglicans tend to favour the Celtic cross or the San Damiano crucifix of Saint Francis. While telling the beads, use a word, a phrase or a sentence from a relevant scriptural text to focus on the image. Touching the fingers on each successive bead, together with the rhythm of the prayers, is another way of stilling the mind. Having completed a round, a period of silence allows you to centre your being in the presence of God.[6]

Handout 42

Bible Study 8: Luke 10.38–42 'Only one thing is needful; Mary has chosen the better part and it is not to be taken away from her.'

We are believers, but we are also members of a particular fellowship or church. Like Martha, we often get distracted by the dogma, politics or busy-ness of the institution. With the best intentions we engage in many pursuits – caring for the church fabric, raising funds, organizing events, singing in the choir, doing good deeds, participating in missionary outreach, etc. But we may well forget that our priority is the living Lord Jesus Christ. Our foremost task is to focus on him in prayer and meditation.

• Share in the group to what extent you may have become preoccupied with things of secondary importance.

Handout 43
Stories and Prayers with Images

In workshops, praying with images has led to a variety of responses. Some people are moved by the story associated with the image, as with Dürer's praying hands, while for others the image can trigger a deeply held personal response, which can be as unexpected as it is profound. Prayers, from over time and place, have been paired with each of the stories but can be used with any other images.

61 – Praying hands

Story 11: Dürer's Praying Hands

As art students, Albrecht Dürer and his friend, Franz Knigstein, worked as casual labourers to try to raise enough money for their studies. But in the economic climate of the time this proved impossible, and so they drew lots as to which of them would find full-time employment to support them both while the other one finished his training. Dürer won and promised Knigstein that he, in turn, would finance his studies.

However, after Dürer had achieved success and returned home to fulfil his promise, he found that it was too late. Through hard labour, Knigstein's fingers had become roughened and bent and he would no longer have the delicate control to handle an artist's brushes. Yet, despite his sacrificial role, Knigstein not only showed no bitterness but was glad to have played his part. One day, Dürer found his friend at prayer. Greatly moved by Knigstein's gnarled hands, he sketched them and later completed one of the great masterpieces of the early Renaissance period. It is a story of love, faith, sacrifice and gratitude. Mother Teresa's prayer embraces all of this and more.

Mother Teresa's Prayer

Light candles in a darkened room and project a series of images from the CD-ROM. Prayer beads and holding crosses can be made available. The prayer is read very slowly by five different readers, with pauses in between to reflect on the projected images. Start with five minutes silence.

Reader 1   Jesus is the Word – to be spoken.
Jesus is the Truth – to be told.
Jesus is the Light – to be lit.
Jesus is the Life – to be lived.
Jesus is the Love – to be loved.

Reader 2   Jesus is the Joy – to be shared.
Jesus is the Peace – to be given.
Jesus is the Bread of Life – to be eaten.
Jesus is the hungry – to be fed.
Jesus is the thirsty – whose thirst is to be quenched.

Reader 3   Jesus is the naked – to be clothed.
Jesus is the homeless – to be taken in.
Jesus is the sick – to be healed.
Jesus is the lonely – to be loved.
Jesus is the unwanted – to be valued.
Jesus is the leper – whose wounds are to be washed.

Reader 4   Jesus is the beggar – to be given a smile.
Jesus is the drunkard – to be listened to.
Jesus is the mentally ill – to be protected.
Jesus is the little one – to be embraced
Jesus is the blind – to be led.
Jesus is the dumb – to be spoken for.

Reader 5   Jesus is the crippled – to be walked alongside.
Jesus is the drug addict – to be befriended.
Jesus is the prostitute – to be removed from danger.
Jesus is the prisoner – to be visited.
Jesus is the elderly – to be served.

Story 12: The Prayer Life of an Inuit Seal-Hunter

At a workshop in British Columbia, Fran Myatt, an Inuit (Eskimo) seal-hunter, was much struck by the image of a Native American Christ at prayer in the Garden of Gethsemane. He was inspired to share something of his own prayer life, which he compared to hunting seals. Sometimes he waited for hours on end and caught nothing, returning home day after day empty-handed. This could continue for a week. Then one day, after only a short time, the seal would come out and he would get it. After carrying it home, nothing would be wasted.

His son was anxious to accompany his father, saying that he was now big and strong enough to help. But Myatt always refused, believing that the boy was not sufficiently patient. He was sure his son would soon get bored, make a noise and sing songs. The seal would hear him and wouldn't come out. For Myatt, this is exactly what his prayer

62 – Native American Christ in the Garden of Gethsemane

life was like. He would wait and wait, and when nothing happened he would get bored, start to sing and make a noise, scaring God's spirit away. At other times, God would draw close, very quietly and give of himself. Myatt said he was no great hunter, yet he hunted. He was no great pray-er either, yet he prayed. The Prayer of St John of the Cross is all about our need for stillness and self-control in our thoughts and actions.

The Prayer of St John of the Cross (1542–91)

O blessed Jesus, give me stillness of soul in Thee.
Let thy mighty calmness reign in me;
Rule me, O King of gentleness, King of peace.
Give me control, great power of self-control,
Control over my words, thoughts and actions.
From all irritability, want of meekness, want of gentleness, dear Lord, deliver
    me.
By thine own deep patience, give me patience.
Make me in this and all things more and more like Thee. Amen.

Story 13: A Latter-Day St Martin

After meditating on the image of a simple crucifix, a Welsh ordinand at the seminary in Cardiff, who had lived in Latin America, told us the story of a poor man in Guatemala who unknowingly followed in the footsteps of St Martin of Tours.

63 – Crucifix

Some communities in Guatemala were celebrating a Mass in solidarity with Nicaraguan Christians who were being persecuted by government forces. During the offertory, every person came up to the altar to leave a gift to be sent to the suffering Church. The poor man's offering was a handful of beans. He was returning to his seat when he stopped, looked round and walked back to the altar. Taking off his jacket, he folded it carefully and left it with the other contributions. The temperature that evening was ten degrees centigrade.[7]

St Martin of Tours (316–97), a monk who became a bishop and a pioneer of Western monasticism, originally joined the Roman army, as had his pagan father before him. But once he became a Christian, he protested at being a soldier and was imprisoned. After his release came the well-known event, immortalized in art, in which he is shown leaning down from his horse, having cut his cloak in half to give it to a cold and starving beggar. Soon afterwards, he had a dream in which Christ appeared to him wearing the cloak.

The *Anima Christi* (the Soul of Christ) is a prayer to Jesus for comfort, strength and guidance and it is often recited by Catholics after receiving Communion. Wrongly attributed to St Ignatius Loyola because of its inclusion in his *Spiritual Exercises*, it dates from the early fourteenth century. Profoundly Christocentric, it is rich in symbols that relate to the Holy Eucharist (Body and Blood of Christ), Baptism (water) and the Passion of Jesus (Holy Wounds).

The Anima Christi

Soul of Christ, sanctify me.
Body of Christ, save me.
Blood of Christ, refresh me.
Water from the side of Christ, wash me.
Passion of Christ, strengthen me.
O good Jesus, hear me.
Within thy wounds hide me.
Suffer me not to be separated from thee.

From the malicious enemy defend me.
In the hour of my death call me.
And bid me to come to thee,
That with all thy saints I may praise thee
For ever and ever. Amen.

Story 14: The Carne Cross

64 – *The Carne Cross*

The story of this image surfaced during a meditation workshop in Winchester.[8] About ten inches high, the cross was made by Lt Col J. P. Carne, VC, DSO, Commander 1st Battalion The Gloucester Regiment, while he was a prisoner of war in North Korea during 1951. Made from grey Korean stone, the cross was painstakingly carved by Carne using two nails and a primitive hammer. Coming from Cornwall, his was a Celtic cross with a circle of stone. Day after day he would sit scraping it smooth on the concrete steps of the schoolhouse in which they were imprisoned. In blessing the cross at their Christmas Communion service, the chaplain prayed: 'May all who look to it with faith and love be given grace to endure unto the end.' Soon afterwards, Carne was subjected to a 'Kangaroo court trial' and underwent a long stint in solitary confinement. The cross is now in Gloucester Cathedral, symbolizing the endurance it represented.

A Celtic Prayer for Protection: Encompassing

The compassing of God be on thee,
   the compassing of the God of life.

The compassing of Christ be on thee,
   the compassing of the Christ of love.

The compassing of the Spirit be on thee,
   the compassing of the Spirit of Grace.

The compassing of the Three be on thee,
   the compassing of the Three preserve thee,
      the compassing of the Three preserve thee. (111, 105)[9]

Handout 44
A Deeper Experience of God

Billy Kennedy, director of the Retreat Centre at Temenos (Sacred Space) in the village of McGregor, finds that many Christians are still uncomfortable with the whole notion of meditation, believing it to be something exotic, if not actually forbidden. What Kennedy appreciates about meditating with images is the essentially non-threatening way in which they allow one to move beyond thought into a deeper silence within oneself and into a deeper experience of God. As he says:

> Meditation requires both a will and a surrendering, allowing the images to sink into the depths of one's being where the Holy Spirit 'does all the work'. A danger with personal spiritual endeavour is that many of us feel that it has to be productive – we have to come away from our practices, prayer meetings and workshops having learnt more. Obviously there is nothing amiss in enriching and extending our knowledge, and a great deal of Christian growth has been inspired in these ways. But one cannot help having the sense that this is just a moistening of the ground. The deeper invitation is always there too. Not only to be open to what God is personally saying to me, but to surrender, much like an image of the Rabbi, who, knowing the Torah by heart, leans his head against the Eastern wall and gives over to silent love.[10]

65 – Holy Spirit dove images

In the extended process of meditation with images, time is put aside in the days that follow to continue reflecting on a chosen image. At some stage, one might feel that one has exhausted the subject, or become bored with it. This is precisely the time to keep going because this is when one can shift gears and enter into the rich life of contemplation, leading to unexpected insights, or a gradual but pervasive change of attitude. For Kennedy: 'The more my reflection on the joy of the Risen Christ becomes part of my being, the more my whole days are lived in the light of it.'[11]

From a psychological point of view, it is possible that just because we do not know why we have chosen a certain image, the time may be ripe for the psyche to open out to the subconscious and reveal untended and unhealed wounds. This journey to healing and wholeness needs to be done safely, with an experienced companion, in the light of Christ. As one begins to move ever deeper into one's inner life, one is guided to bring the light of consciousness into the shadow areas so that one can begin to relate with love and understanding to the whole person.[12]

Handout 45
A Meditative Liturgy

Guidelines for meditation in the liturgy:

- Only one image is projected from the CD-ROM to allow for a concentrated focusing.
- All the participants sit in a semi-circle facing the screen.
- The meditation lasts at least half an hour to make it worthwhile.
- Participants may offer prayerful observations if they feel called by the Spirit to do so, but never exceeding one or two sentences.
- There should be some space between observations and they should refer only to the one image. No comments should be made by others.
- It is perfectly all right to remain silent and say nothing.
- There should be no distractions such as fidgeting, coughing, sighing or looking around.
- Candles, bells and incense may be used.

Liturgy

Leader	You are made in the image of God the Father.
All	We shall be holy as our heavenly Father is holy.
Leader	You are made in the image of Jesus Christ.
All	We shall serve as our Lord has served.
Leader	You are made in the image of the Holy Spirit.
All	We shall be creative as the Spirit is creative.

The Collect

Loving God, who willed into being creation as a living image of your beauty and grandeur; you breathed life into people, male and female, as the crowning image of your wisdom and justice. We ask you to anoint your Church that she may become the image of your healing grace. Amen.

Scripture

An appropriate scripture telling the story of the image is read aloud by a participant.

The Silent Meditation

The meditation formally ends when the Leader reads a prayer chosen for the season.

Leader   May God who invited us to pray for the Kingdom, continue to sustain our prayers, and the blessing of God Almighty – Father, Son and Holy Spirit – be among us and remain with us always. Amen.
Leader   Christ is the Prince of Peace.
All   An everlasting peace beyond words and understanding.

All share the Peace.

Notes

1 Source unknown.

2 Cf. Desmond Tutu, 2004, *God Has a Dream: A Vision of Hope for our Time*, London: Rider, ch. 7.

3 Desmond Tutu, *God Has a Dream*, p. 109.

4 Personal communication. For other ideas on the use of visual images and symbols in prayer see Henry Morgan (ed.), 1991, *Approaches to Prayer: A Resource Book for Groups and Individuals*, London: SPCK, Chs 9 and 10.

5 Information and prayers on the Holding Cross are reproduced by kind permission of Angela Ashwin. Holding crosses are available through the internet and Church bookshops.

6 See Further Resources for internet information on the prayer beads and rosary and their respective prayers.

7 Original source of this story unknown.

8 I am indebted to Ann Lewin, poet and author, for sharing this story. The full version was first published by the chaplain, the Revd S. J. Davies in *The Times*, 20 November 1953.

9 Esther de Waal (ed.), 1988, *The Celtic Vision: Prayers and Blessings from the Outer Hebrides. Selections from the Carmina Gadelica*, London: Darton, Longman and Todd, p. 161.

10 Personal communication.

11 Personal communication.

12 Personal communication.

7

'AFRAID TO LOOK AT GOD!'

66 – Jesus Christ Superstar

Introductory Talk: Seeing Jesus Anew

'Moses hid his face as he was afraid to look at God.' (Exodus 3.6)

It is easy to fall into the trap of thinking that religious art would by its very nature have a profound spiritual impact. But, in reality, such imagery can have the opposite effect by merely confirming our stereotypes and preconceptions. Work that challenges and surprises is far more likely to open our eyes as to how people see Jesus and stimulate discussion, as has been our workshop experience. It might also explain the popularity of exhibitions of Christian art since the Millennium, sparking off a wave of interest even to those of other faiths or none. This interest has been sustained. Contrast such enthusiasm with the steady decline in fervour for religious practice and one has some idea of the spiritual hunger that is waiting to be assuaged through visual imagery, symbol and myth.

Coinciding with the Millennial celebrations, churches, cathedrals and art galleries throughout the country had people flocking in record-breaking numbers to exhibitions of 'How We See Jesus'. During 2001, the 'Seeing Salvation' exhibition in the National Gallery in London attracted thousands of people and many more watched the series on television. Neil McGregor, who curated the exhibition, believes that the enduring fascination for many people is in seeing how artists have grappled with the paradoxes of faith that have shaped European culture over the centuries: 'From early Christians in the Roman catacombs to Salvador Dali (they) have tackled the problem of showing Christ as both human and divine, as both victim and conqueror: one man, but the whole of humanity.'[1]

McGregor reminds us that Jesus and his Jewish followers would have recoiled from the idea of any image of the divine. Nor were the first Christians interested in how Jesus looked. What mattered was what he did – as their Saviour. Only later, as the Church's devotion focused more on the person of Jesus, did visual images become important. McGregor argues that, even though Gospel texts leave us free to imagine how Jesus looked, artists depicting him over the centuries have had to decide on a particular image, doing theology in the process. Furthermore, by universalizing particular events in the life of Christ, the artist is able to relate them to our human experience, from birth to death. This archetypal imagery is what touches people so deeply. But, as McGregor says, in each generation the problem remains of how to represent Christ so that he becomes a living reality.[2] McGregor's concern is with western European religious imagery, but these same issues are just as pertinent in other cultures.

Over the centuries, the Church has been the main patron of religious works and continues to play a significant role. The travelling exhibition of the Methodist Church Collection of Modern Christian Art is one example.[3] The flood of contemporary Stations of the Cross, stained-glass windows and crucifixes in churches around the country is another, as are the often contentious works of art displayed in cathedrals such as Chichester, Lincoln and Coventry. In 2009, Chichester Cathedral held a competition in memory of Dean Walter Hussey, to create an installation in the space above the Arundel screen, with five international artists submitting their designs.

The Art and Christianity Enquiry (ACE) provides a forum for debate about displaying contemporary visual art in sacred spaces, while museums and art galleries play their part too, as in the Art of Faith exhibition in Norwich Castle,

Norfolk, with religious artworks from the Bronze Age to the present. Recently, the National Gallery mounted an exhibition 'The Sacred Made Real: Spanish Painting and Sculpture 1600–1700', with numerous images of Christ by artists such as Velazquez and Zurbaran. Of note was the artists' zeal in seeking realism with glass eyes and tears, real teeth and simulations of clotted blood for the crucifixion. The sculptures are still an integral part of people's faith in churches and processions.[4]

Nowadays, ignorance of the Christian tradition is another sort of challenge. As in the Middle Ages, when clergy used paintings to teach the Christian faith to a largely illiterate following, so has the latest technology become an educational tool. The 'Images of Salvation' project, carried out jointly by St John's College, Nottingham and the University of York, produced a CD-ROM with a selection of medieval art as a way of introducing the Bible to undergraduates.

Handout 46
Programme for 'Afraid to Look at God'

Workshops, from Handout 46, can be selected according to the nature of the event (a one-off workshop, part of a course or day-long programme), the images or films available and time constraints. Refreshments are provided as required.

Programme for 'Afraid to Look at God'

15 minutes:	Introductory talk: Seeing Jesus Anew.
c. 1½ hours:	*Handout 47: 'Images that Shock or Offend'.*
	Exercise 15: Images that Shock or Offend.
c. 45 minutes:	*Handout 48: Images from South Africa.*
	Story 15: 'Jesus Suffering from AIDS'.
	Story 16: 'The Broken Christ'.
	Exercise 16: 'Stories from South Africa'.
c. 1 hour:	*Handout 49: Jesus in Advertising.*
	Exercise 17: 'Christian Iconography in Commercial Advertising'.
	Exercise 18: 'Christian Advertising'.
Variable:	*Handout 50: The Celluloid Jesus.*
	Exercise 19: 'Jesus in Film'.
	Exercise 20: 'The Christ Figure in Film'.
30 minutes:	*Handout 51: Bible study: John 20.11–16.*

Handout 47
Images that Shock or Offend

In a workshop, some images of Christ may shock or offend, as in the illustration below. Reasons given range from their being too sentimental or distasteful; to romanticizing the gospel story; to their being downright heretical or obscene.

67 – Christ as a Latin American revolutionary

Even so, such iconography can provoke profound theological discussion and raise issues which might have been ignored.

Cooper suggests that if the purpose of the images is simply to enable discussion of theological ideas that already exist, then the quality of art doesn't matter. However, if we are looking to artists to enable new ways of experiencing and encountering God, then the art has to be correspondingly deep. Thus, 'both "good" artists and "good" poets go intuitively beyond the horizon that presents a barrier to intellectual reasoning, blazing a trail for the thinkers, who catch up later'.[5]

Cathedrals have certainly taken this view, displaying images that have caused an outcry but also initiated serious debate. For example, when Leonard McComb's nude sculpture, 'Young Man Standing', was displayed in Lincoln Cathedral in 1990, the upset was such that it was withdrawn. In 1996, Bill Viola's video installation in Durham Cathedral of a nude figure moving continuously through water necessitated the screening off of the display. However, many people interpreted these as images of Christ.

Michele Coxton's sculpture 'The Naked Christ' was inspired by Michelangelo's fifteenth-century crucifix of that name. Her materials were garnered from her Welsh countryside: bones of dead sheep picked clean by crows and foxes, water-worn wood and rusted metal left by farmers. Her intention was 'to sculpt the image of a man who has suffered and whose earthly body is decaying, like the animals on my walks. The soul has flown, but only just.'[6] The sculpture was displayed in Shrewsbury Abbey in 2001 and, despite controversy, remained there for three years. People either hated it or loved it; but it served its purpose in providing a challenging statement on the death of Christ.

Such images have fuelled a furious debate about the relationship between modern art and religion. The director of the Bowes Museum, Barnard Castle, cites their paintings of Jesus Christ stapled to a cross as an example: 'We have to make a decision whether (such images are) simply gratuitous or not. You have to strike a balance. Contemporary art knows it's going to get knocked, but if it causes debate then it is doing its job.'[7] Both artists and art-viewers can invoke self-censorship, but it is becoming harder to shock the public.

In 2004, the Chinese-born artist, Terence Koh, caused a furore in a Baltic Centre exhibition in Gateshead, with his foot-high plaster statue of Christ, with an erection. Despite warning signs, visitors and church leaders accused the gallery of showing disrespect to the Christian faith. One woman, who had only seen the media coverage, tried to take the gallery to court for offending public decency, but got nowhere.[8]

Two works by Paul Fryer, exhibited in the former Holy Trinity Church in central London, now One Marylebone, of waxworks of a black Jesus being electrocuted and a crucified ape, also hit the headlines. For Fryer, the gorilla artwork 'is a reminder of our collective responsibility to protect those who are least able to protect themselves', while the Jesus sculpture was designed to get visitors thinking about how he died. Some might have been shocked, but these images were intended 'to inspire people to think and understand "deeper meanings"'.[9]

Gormley's series of crucified effigies, moulded on his body and displayed along the walls of Londonderry as a symbol of sectarian strife, might seem tame after this, as is the prize-winning *Spectrum Jesus* by Keith Coventry, inspired by the work of a Dutch art forger.[10] However, it is the Jewish Museum of Art in London that mounted a most surprising exhibition: 'The Cross Purposes – Shock and Contemplation in Images of the Crucifixion'. It offers a visual representation of how the crucifixion has changed over time – from solely Christian to a more generic expression of suffering, with Tracy Emin exhibited alongside Graham Sutherland. Many in the Jewish community found it highly contentious.[11]

Exercise 15: Images that Shock or Offend

- What images of Christ would you find offensive and why?
- Do you think such images have a 'deeper meaning' and could initiate a constructive debate? Are they disrespectful to the Christian faith?

Handout 48
Images from South Africa

Story 15: Jesus Suffering from AIDS

The images from South Africa are of a different order. A recent UNAIDS report estimated that 12 per cent of that country's population of 48 million was infected with HIV/AIDS, the highest incidence in the world. Most prevalent among young female adults, many babies are born with the infection, and the number of orphans and child-headed households has risen alarmingly. Yet, when a painting of *Jesus Suffering from AIDS* was exhibited in St George's Cathedral, Cape Town, in 1994, the press was inundated with righteous complaints.

68 – Christ, the Healer

In September 2010, the Revd Xola Skosana, pastor of the non-denominational Way of Life Church in Khayelitsha, a township outside Cape Town with a high HIV infection rate, added to the controversy by claiming that Jesus was an AIDS victim. This was not meant literally, but was his way of saying that Jesus is with the wounded and the suffering. Many were encouraged to be more open about their status and overcome their fear of stigma. Others were outraged by his undergoing an HIV test during a church service. Christians worldwide accused this courageous man of calling Jesus sexually promiscuous, they having failed to understand his message completely.

Story 16: The Broken Christ

The other South African story harks back to the time of the liberation struggle, but the issues remain pertinent in many parts of the world today. A photo taken in the 1980s shows a shattered crucifix lying face-down on the floor, arms broken, in St Joseph's Catholic Church, Phokeng. At the time the Church was becoming increasingly involved in non-violent action, and the bomb blast which caused the damage was almost certainly instigated by the apartheid regime. The shocking part is that the perpetrators would have been ardent churchgoers, used to family prayers and daily Bible-reading.

Exercise 16: Stories from South Africa

- Do you agree with presenting Jesus as HIV positive? Why?

- As you contemplate the struggle for justice in South Africa, how does an image of Jesus with broken arms strike you?

69 – The Rich Young Ruler

Handout 49
Jesus in Advertising

There is no doubting the power of visual imagery to communicate a message. However, the use of Christian iconography does not necessarily equal Christian intent. What is puzzling is why advertisers use religious images to promote their wares in a secular context. If the role of advertising is to add value to a product by investing it with meaning, then why spend vast sums of money in using Christian iconography?

Shock tactics seem to be a significant element, assuming that consumers are sufficiently informed to be shocked, or else enjoy a joke at the Church's expense. In advertisements, Jesus has been co-opted into promoting anything from cool drinks, alcohol, music, paper, car repairs and ethical treatment of animals ('Jesus was a Vegetarian', with an orange slice for a halo), to women's clothing and fashion jewellery. A picture of Raquel Welch in a leather bikini strapped to a cross caused some fury, as did a magazine cover headed 'The Resurrection of David Beckham', with the footballer festooned with crucifixes and rosaries and arms outstretched.

Christmas advertisements have used humour as a selling point. For example, the Heineken poster showing a Nativity scene with Joseph shouting: 'It's a girl'; the Tango advert with two kneeling children praying for the soft drink; a paper company basing all its slogans on the Nativity ('Behold! The King of paper is born', etc.); and a Bulgarian winery linking its modest beginnings to the fact that 'Jesus was born in a trough'.

However, when the *Sunday Times* magazine blazoned the message: 'This Sunday read the Bible. *Style*, the new bible of fashion and fitness. Worship it every Sunday', one might well ask, 'What is going on here?' If secular imagery has supplanted the historical dominance of religious imagery, why do advertisers invest so much in Christian imagery? The number of complaints must be considered too few to count, except that the Heineken advert was withdrawn. What is the marketing ploy, which the Church seems to have missed?

In fact, the Church's Advertising Network (CAN), ChurchAds.Net, is an ecumenical charity that has tapped into this potential with its striking Christmas and Easter posters. By co-opting the power of popular images and language, it has tried to communicate a more contemporary message. Their unambiguous purpose is to reach the 'unreached' and those on the fringe of the Church, using bus-stops and bill-boards for their publicity.

CAN started cautiously in 1991 with a poster inviting people to 'Give Jesus a birthday present – wrap up the kids and take them to church'. Gradually, the copy got more provocative, as with the 1999 poster, 'Meek. Mild. As if.', comparing Che Guevera with Jesus as Revolutionary Hero. Despite the uproar, this was a serious attempt to invest Jesus with features symbolic of modern struggles and ideologies. The trendy imagery of another poster declared: 'Bad Hair Day?! You're a virgin, you've just given birth and now three kings have shown up. Make room for God this Christmas'. The idea was to relate Christ's usage of parable to people's present experience. Similarly, in 2010 the campaign image was a 'Baby Scan Jesus' with the words 'He's on his way. Christmas starts with Christ'. Here, the coming birth of Jesus is identified with the popular convention in which proud parents-to-be show off scans of their expected baby. In contrast, the usual church advertising was said to be more likely 'hand-written in felt-tip pen, flapping desperately in the wind behind cling-film or in a freezer bag'.[12]

In the United States, a church in Maryland bucked the soft-sell approach by showing a historic crucifixion scene with the words scratched over it: 'Of course people with pierced body parts are welcome in our church'. Birmingham Diocese caused an uproar by following suit with a poster saying 'Body Piercing? Jesus had this done 2,000 years ago'. An analysis of this imagery might well open up new avenues for mission.

In preparation for both exercises, the group needs to collect commercial and religious advertisements in magazines, newspapers, posters

70 – Che Guevara – Jesus as revolutionary hero

(including ChurchAds.net), Alpha publicity, etc., in which Christian iconography is used either to sell products or to attract people to church.

Exercise 17: Christian Iconography in Commercial Advertising

- Why do you think advertisers invest money in using Christian iconography to sell their products in a secular world? What is the potential marketing ploy?
- How do such advertisements challenge your faith?

Exercise 18: Christian Advertising

- Do you think the CAN advertisements communicate a more contemporary message of the Christian faith?
- Why do you think CAN posters have created so much controversy among British churchgoers?

Handout 50
The Celluloid Jesus

This is an extensive genre, as internet references show, but can only be touched on here. Cinematic representations of Christ vary from the big-budget historical epics, such as *King of Kings* (1961), and Mel Gibson's *The Passion of the Christ* (2004); to the didactic, which adheres more closely to contemporary scholarship, as in Franco Zeffirelli's *Jesus of Nazareth* (1977). Others raise contemporary issues through symbol and allegory, as in Denys Arcand's *Jesus of Montreal* (1989), while in *The Last Temptation of Christ* (1988), Martin Scorsese presents a fictional exploration of the inner struggle between Christ's divine and human natures, which some regarded as

71 – Christ, the Hollywood hero

heretical. Like the artists, all reflect a personal interpretation of Christ's life and ministry, but on a much larger scale determined by financial considerations.[13]

Exercise 19: Jesus in Film

What do you look for in a film about Jesus – historical accuracy, popular appeal, educational interest, controversial material that raises questions, inspirational content, comparisons with contemporary issues and conflicts – or what else?

- Having looked at one of the films listed in Further Resources, how would you rate it as a film critic, from 0 to 5 stars? What criteria have influenced your decision? Has it given you any new insights?
- What impact would the film make on a non-believer?

The Christ Figure is a spiritual or prophetic person who in some way reflects or parallels Christ's life. This could be in terms of sheer goodness, performing miracles, healing people, fighting for justice, being loving and forgiving, withdrawing into the wilderness, undertaking sacrificial acts of courage, re-enacting a crucifixion, etc. Such figures can be found in films like *The Shawshank Redemption*, *The Matrix Trilogy*, *Babette's Feast*, *Dead Man Walking*, *Lord of the Flies*, *One Flew Over the Cuckoo's Nest*, *The Mission*, *The Miracle Worker*, *A Man for All Seasons*, *Schindler's List* and many more, including Disney cartoons.

Exercise 20: The Christ Figure in Film

Participants are asked to bring clips of such films followed by discussion.

- Why could this person be regarded as a Christ figure?
- What effect did he or she have in other people's lives?

Handout 51

Bible Study 9: John 20.11–16

Looking for Jesus' body, Mary Magdalene sees somebody outside the holy tomb. It is Jesus, but in her confusion she fails to recognize him. Mary thinks she is talking to a gardener, possibly the resident tomb-caretaker. Otherwise, she would not have said: 'If you have carried him away, tell me where you have laid him.' Only when Jesus reveals himself does she recognize him. She is shocked to discover her Lord disguised in this way.

Likewise, Jesus meets us in various unseemly situations but, as he is hidden, we fail to encounter him and pass him by.

- Discuss various situations where we are shocked by the revelation of the crucified Christ, as in some images or films.

72 – African Madonna

Handout 52
Programme for Women Re-imaging Christ

Workshops are selected from Handout 52 as required.

Programme for Women Re-imaging Christ

	Prayer of Lady Julian of Norwich
c. 1 hour:	*Handout 53: Women Re-imaging Christ*
	Exercise 21: 'Women Re-imaging Christ'
c. 1 hour:	*Handout 54: Jesa Christa Crucified*
	Exercise 22: 'Feminine Images of Christ's Passion'
Variable:	*Handout 55: A Liturgy Celebrating the Motherhood of Christ*
	– 'Woman: An Image of Christ Worthy of Honour'.

Prayer of Lady Julian of Norwich (1342–*c.* 1416)

Lord God, I understand three ways of contemplating your motherhood.
The first is the creation of our human nature.
The second is your taking on of our nature where your motherhood of grace begins.
The third is your motherhood at work in that, by your grace, everything is penetrated in length and in breadth, in height and in depth, without end; and it is all in love. Amen.[14]

Handout 53
Women Re-imaging Christ

Hildegard of Bingen (*c.* 1098–1179)

Since Jesus took his body from a virgin woman, it is woman rather than man who best represents the humanity of the Son of God.

No matter their colour or condition, from the earliest times women everywhere have suffered exclusion within a patriarchal Church. Feminine models of spirituality recorded in the Scriptures have long been ignored, as in Isaiah and in the accounts of Jesus' mutually enriching encounters with women. It was many years before some brave souls discarded traditional images of Christ, which perpetuated their oppression, and discovered him anew for themselves. In so doing they found freedom and self-respect in coming to a fresh understanding of their worth as well as their faith.

Both men and women artists use Christological symbols to explore the suffering of women, or their nurturing role as mother. For example, in his *Resurrection, Cookham*, Stanley Spencer depicts Christ in a maternal role, cradling babies in his arms. So, too, women's images of a male Christ have their own authenticity, coming as they do from their womanist theological perspective. In Asia, such images represent 'a Christological transformation created out of Asian women's experiences as they struggle for full humanity'.[15] This can be said for women across the world.

This is exemplified in a series of paintings by Coral Bernadine in St Michael's Roman Catholic Church Centre, Black Rock, Barbados. In her portrayal of *Survivors of the Middle Passage* (1992), she celebrates her forebears who resisted colonial oppression, from slaves triumphantly breaking their chains to modern heroes of the freedom movement, like Martin Luther King, Harriet Tubman and Bob Marley. This womanist black consciousness permeates all her art. In *The Crucifixion*, a dark-skinned Jesus is surrounded by cameos of him healing the sick, cleansing the Temple and rising in glory. Her trademark Isaiahan image has a lion lying down with a lamb below (see image on CD-ROM). In her portrayal of Mary as *Mother of the Oppressed* (early 1990s), a matronly Caribbean Madonna is enthroned in heavenly splendour. The resurrected Jesus, stigmata visible on his palms, looks up as he grasps the hand of a naked, skeletal figure, symbolizing his compassion for and identification with, the suffering of black people. Again, heroes of the liberation struggle fill the picture including Nelson Mandela.

Many of the revolutionary Nicaraguan artists in *The Gospel in Art by the Peasants of Solentiname* were also women. In their brightly coloured paintings, their faith in 'the living word of the living God' is incarnated in the context of their island home. Jesus is portrayed as a poor *campesino* like them. His story is re-enacted in the dramatic events of the people's struggle against the ravages of Somoza's National Guard in 1977. It is a powerful testimony to the enduring hope of a persecuted people in the good news of the Kingdom.[16]

This Christology resonates with the Manchurian artist, Taeko Tomiyama, who became actively involved in politics during the labour strikes of 1960. For her, a painting is not just a beautiful object to be admired, but must provoke the viewer to action.[17] Her powerful painting of the *Pieta of Kwangju* (*The Christ We Share*, no. 29) was inspired by the brutal suppression of the people in this Korean city by military forces. The women's plight is vividly captured in Mary's grief, with a single large tear coursing down her cheek as she cradles Jesus' head in her lap. A wailing figure kneels behind. The agony of the event is intensified by depicting the figures in black and white against a blood-red background.

In Australia's Northern Territory, Miriam-Rose Ungunmerr trespassed into the aboriginal male world by painting a series of Stations of the Cross for her church using traditional stylistic patterns and ancient symbols to express inner meanings (*The Christ We Share*, no. 20). Another Australian, Margaret Ackland, is equally innovative in having women and children, including a breast-feeding mother, seated alongside men in her *Last Supper* (1993), 'serving to amplify and make present the symbols of this meal of nourishment and hope'.[18]

In Britain, Dinah Roe Kendall and Gillian Bell Richards excel at giving new life and meaning to the Gospel story as it is re-enacted in the context of their contemporary surroundings. In contrast, Sarah Lucas's crucified Christ made out of cigarettes, and Sam Taylor Wood's photographic depiction of Da Vinci's *Last Supper*, entitled *Wrecked* (1996), with a bare-breasted woman replacing the figure of Christ, aim to challenge traditional symbolic imagery.

Two American artists have managed to capture the sheer humanity of Jesus. Janet McKenzie's *Jesus of the People* has the haunting image of a youthful Native American Jesus flanked by indigenous symbols, while Marylyn Felion's watercolour of *Christ as Poor, Black, Deathrow Inmate*, is of a prisoner whom she accompanied to the electric chair in Nebraska in 1997, 'the most God-filled person' whom she ever knew.[19]

Exercise 21: Women Re-imaging Christ

Pick an image from the book, or the CD-ROM, with a womanist theme and discuss the following:

- How does the image challenge your understanding of the nature of Jesus?
- Compare and contrast how the same image affects men and women in the group.

Handout 54
Jesa Christa Crucified

Some of the most powerful statements by women artists in the West have been their re-imaging of Christ as a crucified woman, with or without the cross and usually naked. These often controversial images raise questions as to how we relate to our body and of how women find healing in identifying with the Passion of Christ.

The theological concept of Jesa Christa crucified is about female figures taking on the kenotic or self-emptying persona of Jesus. One may see the figure of Jesa Christa as a theological statement about the pristine nature of Christ transcending and embracing both male and female forms. The masculinity of Jesus is not an inalienable part of his humanity. God did not become a man *per se*. He became human. Women extend Jesus' humanity to include femininity. Jesa Christa crucified can also

73 – Jesa Christa crucified

be seen as the radical revelation of the suffering of women, which is redemptive and transformative. In that sense it is more than a political re-imaging of a male Jesus evoking pity and outrage. It is a sacred image of transcendence relevant to the spirituality of both sexes although, as an icon, it exclusively tells the story of women. (See images on CD-ROM.)

Investing a woman with divinity is already making a statement about the divine becoming vulnerable. In 1984, the American sculptor, James Murphy, created a two-foot figure of a woman, hands and feet nailed to a cross, which unapologetically represented a female crucifixion. Entitled, *Christine on the Cross*, he was inspired by the realization that 'the world's rejection and hatred of women culminates in crucifying the female Christ'.[20] Since then, women themselves have set their own imprint on the imaging of Jesa Christa crucified, with newly won perspectives feeding in to their contextualization of theology through art.

In 1974, Edwina Sandys, American granddaughter of Winston Churchill, sculpted her *Christa* for the United Nations Decade of Women. The bronze is of a nude female, with head drooping and arms outstretched on a cross. For Sandys, she represented 'any women forgotten, hidden, abused, or thrown away', as in prisons – 'the suffering of women in all of us' in general and in women, in particular (*The Christ We Share*, no. 30). When the sculpture was exhibited in the

Episcopal Cathedral of St John the Divine, New York, in 1984, some thought it 'a desecration', but the whole idea was to force people to think theologically, to show the power and the vulnerability of the Christ in each one of us.

A similar seven-foot bronze, *Crucified Woman*, by Almuth Lutkenhaus-Lackey, was even more controversial. Created in 1976, the naked, female figure is in cruciform shape with arms outstretched. There is no cross because for many women their lives are a perpetual crucifixion. The ballet-like pose evokes a resurrection theme, comparable with the image of the dancing risen Christ in Asian Christology. But the beauty of the youthful body is in painful contrast to the sorrowing, scarred face. First shown in a United Church in Toronto, the sculpture was later moved to the grounds of Emmanuel theological college. Although it was vilified by some as heretical, even erotic, it forced many people to grapple with issues at the heart of women's theology, transforming them in the process. In identifying their struggles and suffering with the sculpture, a cross-section of women were freed to talk about their faith, often for the first time, and found healing and wholeness in the process.[21]

74 – Crucified woman

In her photo of *Yo Mama's Last Supper*, in New York's Brooklyn Museum, Renee Cox depicts Christ as a beautiful, nude woman, a long white cloth draped over her outstretched arms. She invites us to the Passover Feast set before her, prefiguring Christ's crucifixion. Shockingly different is *Bosnian Christa* created by the British artist, Margaret Argyle, in mixed textiles, in 1993. Here, the image of a women's open vulva, all in red, frames the slender profile of a nude, crucified woman against a cross. The Christian imagery of a bleeding vulva tellingly symbolizes the rape of Muslim women during the Bosnian War and the brutalization of women across the religious and cultural spectrum.

The story of Maria Cristina Gomez, a Baptist primary school teacher from El Salvador, epitomizes the lot of Latin American women in their striving for justice. Her crime was to belong to a Base Christian Community, who put their faith into action in their peasant communities. In 1989, she was abducted by armed men, tortured and killed: her martyrdom taking on the persona of the kenotic

Christ. Her friends commissioned a painted wooden cross to celebrate all the aspects of her life and faith. (*The Christ We Share*, no. 3)

Mary, the mother of Christ, is another female figure who is symbolically identified with Jesa Christa crucified. In *The Power and the Glory*, Coral Bernadine depicts Mary as a fulsomely breasted, bare-footed Caribbean mother in faded, tattered clothing. Surrounded by exotic food and vegetation, with the sea beyond, Mary stands open-armed in front of the crucified Christ, his blood trickling over her large, rough working hands. Christ's eucharistic sacrifice is symbolized by a Bible, wine and home-baked bread on a table alongside, with the church altar behind. In identifying with the broken body of Christ, this humble Mary is transformed into a priestly figure, who has

75 – The Power and the Glory

the power to consecrate, sanctify and bless creation, welcoming in the abundance of the Kingdom.

Lastly, the use of Christological imagery to represent the feminine categories of motherland and earth is well illustrated in *Birhen ng Balintawak – Our Lady Virgin of Balintawak*. This image of the Madonna and Child is an icon of the Philippine Independent Church, affiliated to the Anglican Communion, and is filled with revolutionary symbols, signifying their long struggle to overcome exploitation from successive colonizers. Santo Nino, the Holy Child, is dressed as a triumphant Katapunan guerrilla, representing the peasants' fight for freedom. The Virgin's gown displays the banned colours of the Filipino flag, symbolizing the Motherland, a feminine category, personifying the figure of Jesa Christa herself.

Exercise 22: Feminine Images of Christ's Passion

- List feminine categories which may be personified by the image of Jesa Christa.
- Discuss how and why many women find healing through identifying with feminine images of the Passion of Christ.

Handout 55
A Liturgy Celebrating the Motherhood of Christ

Project images of, or by, women or, alternatively, use a display of such images.

Leader	There is neither East nor West,
All	in Christ Jesus.
Leader	There is neither black nor white,
All	in Christ Jesus.
Leader	There is neither male nor female,
All	in Christ Jesus.

Hymn

'Brother, sister, let me serve you' (Richard Gillard, b. 1953).

Scripture

Luke 15.8–10; John 4.6–30.

Talk: Woman: an Image of Christ Worthy of Honour

The woman looking for a lost coin and rejoicing over finding it is a women-friendly metaphor for God responding similarly to the restoration of one lost soul. God is the caring, nurturing, sheltering mother energy. That was how God was perceived by Pandita Ramabai (1858–1922), a high-caste Brahmin woman born in India, who came to Christ on reading the story of Jesus' encounter with the Samaritan woman in the Gospel of Luke. She was struck by the gentle way in which Jesus engaged the lowly woman in a dialogue, as equals. Ramabai claimed that Jesus was her Saviour and the Saviour of millions of her oppressed Indian sisters.

Once, Ramabai had a clay image of Jesus made to be installed in the shrine of her hostel, which sheltered homeless women: child widows, reformed sex workers, temple dancing girls and abused young women. While the image was being transported, its arms fell off. Many considered it an ill omen. But Ramabai told the women: 'Jesus without his arms is telling us something here. He wants us to be his arms, working through us and investing us with his power. Each one of you women is an image of Jesus. Each one of you has the light of Christ within you.'

Reflect on the story in a few moments of silence, followed by a prayer:

Prayer

Compassionate God, you rejoice over the redemption of one lost soul just as the woman rejoiced over the finding of her lost coin. Hold us ever close to your bosom and empower us with your motherly healing. Amen.

Leader	Merciful God, shelter us from all adversities and nourish us with the milk of your divine grace; and the blessing of God – Creator, Redeemer and Comforter – rest upon us and abide with us for ever. Amen.
Leader	Let us share the peace of Christ.
All	Even the peace which follows justice. Halleluiah.

All share the Peace.

Notes

1 Neil McGregor, 'How We See Jesus', *The Daily Telegraph*, 19 February 2000.

2 Neil McGregor, 'How We See Jesus'.

3 Roger Wollen, 2004, *The Methodist Church Collection of Modern Christian Art: An Introduction*, Peterborough: Methodist Publishing House; www. methodist.org.uk/ artcollection/ and *A Guide to the Methodist Art Collection* (2010), available from www.mph. org.uk.

4 Miguel de Santiago, 'Spanish Religious Art in London', published in *Razon y Fe* magazine, 2009, www.razonyfe.es.

5 Personal communication.

6 See   http://www.nakedchrist.co.uk/reaction/shrew-chron-010404.html;   http://www. nakedchrist.co.uk/sculpture.html.

7 'Art and the Power to Shock', *Northern Echo*, 25 February 2004.

8 See articles in webmaster@religiouswatch.com; news.bbc.co.uk; dailymail.co.uk; entertainment.timesonline.co.uk.

9 Andrew Hough, 14 October 2009, http://www.telegraph.co.uk/culture/art/art-news/ 6319258.

10 *ArtsHub*, 22 September 2010.

11 Louise Jury, *London Evening Standard*, 10 June 2010.

12 Richard Ellis cited by Andrew Carey, 'Tearing their hair out', *Church of England Newspaper*, 13 March 1998.

13 See, for example: Lloyd Baugh, 1997, *Imaging the Divine. Jesus and Christ-Figures in Film*, Kansas City, MO: Sheed and Ward; Roy Kinnard and Tim Davis, 1992, *Divine Images: A History of Jesus on the Screen*, New York: Citadel Press; Richard C. Stern, Clayton Jefford, Guerric Dibona, 1999, *Savior of the Silver Screen*, New Jersey: Paulist Press.

14 *Showings* (first published in 1670 – modern English version), chapter 59.

15 Chung Hyun Kyung, 1990, *Struggle to be the Sun Again: Introducing Asian Women's Theology*, Maryknoll: Orbis Books, p. 62.

16 Philip and Sally Scharper (eds), 1984, *The Gospel in Art by the Peasants of Solentiname*, Maryknoll: Orbis Books.

17 Masao Takenaka and Ron O'Grady, 1991, *The Bible Through Asian Eyes*, Auckland: Pace Publishing with Asian Christian Art Association, p. 154.

18 Ron O'Grady, 2001, *Christ for All People: Celebrating a World of Christian Art*, Geneva: WCC Publications, pp. 102–3.

19 Ron O'Grady, *Christ for All People*, pp. 30–1, 107.

20 Doris Jean Dyke, 1991, *Crucified Woman*, Toronto: United Church Publishing House, p. 41.

21 Doris Jean Dyke, *Crucified Woman*, pp. 3–9, 15, 29–30, 63–74.

POSTSCRIPT

In working with images of Christ we travel the globe, visiting people of faith and encountering the incarnate Christ who is liberated from the shackles with which we have bound him. We do not need to be holy or religious to relate to an image. Nor do we need to be highly educated or have theological expertise. We may belong to a church or not. The Christ who comes to us through images is not the Christ of the academe, but the visible Christ with whom we can interact. We become our own theologians and take responsibility for our own journeys of faith. We discover our own Christologies, not in any abstract, intellectual way, but by reaching in to the multidimensional diversity incarnate in the images.

Through the images, we, the people of God, are empowered to explore our relationship with the mystery of Christ, individually and collectively. The focus of our meditation and reflection is not the Jesus of history or eternity, but the Jesus of the here and now, who is forever touching and transforming our lives. This ever newly incarnated Jesus, endowed with many faces, comes to us as the Saviour who offers inexhaustible future possibilities. He affirms every context, allowing peoples of the world to meet him in their unique stories. He is the Jesus of as many Christologies as there are contexts.

As a celebration of the completion of the manuscript, a private exhibition was held of Ann Snaddon's illustrations in my home in McGregor. Although it was not advertised, over 50 people came and continued coming for the next few days. Most were not churchgoers, and some claimed no religious beliefs. Yet they stayed to talk about the images and even share their faith among themselves. This was a truly missionary event without any church trappings. It was a real vindication of the educational and spiritual value of sacred images in the life of a community.

The Christ we discover in and through the images challenges us to go out into the world and incarnate the selfsame Christ in every situation, wherever that may be. It is a journey from meditation to proclamation and praxis. This is what mission is all about. This is what 'seeing our faith' is all about.

FURTHER RESOURCES

Jesus in Art

Jane Alison (ed.), n.d., *Stanley Spencer. The Apotheosis of Love*, Exhibition Catalogue, London: Barbican Art Gallery.

Peter E. Ball, 1999, *Icons of the Invisible God*, Newark: Chevron Books. For a list of commissions in church buildings: www.petereugeneball.com.

Barbara Burn (compiler), (1989), *The Life of Christ: Images from the Metropolitan Museum of Art*, London, New York: Barrie & Jenkins, Museum.

Chinese Artists, 1943 (reprinted 1961), *The Life of Christ*, London: SPG.

Frans Claerhout, 1998, *It Could Happen Here*, Bloemfontein: Dreyer Publishers.

Helen De Borchgrave, 1999, *A Journey into Christian Art*, Oxford: Lion.

George Ferguson, 1954, *Signs and Symbols in Christian Art: With Illustrations from Paintings from the Renaissance*, USA: Oxford University Press.

Gabriele Finaldi *et al.*, 2000, *The Image of Christ: Seeing Salvation* exhibition catalogue, National Gallery, London, New Haven: Yale University Press.

Timothy Hyman and Patrick Wright (eds), 2001, *Stanley Spencer* exhibition catalogue, London: Tate Publishing.

Images of Christ: Religious Iconography in Twentieth Century British Art, 1993, London: exhibition in St Matthew's Church, Northampton and St Paul's Cathedral, London.

Dinah Roe Kendall, 2002, *Allegories of Heaven: An Artist Explores the 'Greatest Story Ever Told'*, Carlisle: Piquant.

William Kurulek, 1976, *A Northern Nativity: Christmas Dreams of a Prairie Boy*, New York: Tundra Books.

Jill Liddell, 1993, *The Patchwork Pilgrimage*, New York: Viking Studio Books.

Gennadios Limouris, 1990, *Windows on Eternity: Theology and Spirituality in Colour*, Geneva: WCC Publications.

Eric Newton, 1966, *The Christian Faith in Art*, London: Thames & Hudson.

Robert Cummings North, 2001, *Symbols of Jesus: A Christology of Symbolic Engagement*, Cambridge: Cambridge University Press.

Ron O'Grady, 2001, *Christ For All People: Celebrating a World of Christian Art*, Geneva: WCC Publications.

J. R. Porter, 1999, *Jesus Christ. The Jesus of History, the Christ of Faith*, London: Duncan Baird.

Rembrandt Bible Drawings, 1979, New York: Dover Publications Inc.

S. I. Robinson, 1996, *Images of Byzantium: Learning about Icons*, London: Loizou Publications.

Philip and Sally Scharper (eds), 1984, *The Gospel in Art by the Peasants of Solentiname*, Maryknoll: Orbis Books.

Son of Man: Pictures and Carvings by Indian, African and Chinese artists, 1939 (reprinted 1962), London: SPG.

Masao Takenaka, 1975, *Christian Art in Asia*, Japan: Kyo Bun Kwan with Christian Conference of Asia.

Masao Takenaka and Ron O'Grady, 1991, *The Bible Through Asian Eyes*, Auckland: Pace Publishing with Asian Christian Art Association.

Alfred Thomas, 1948 (reprinted 1961), *The Life of Christ by an Indian Artist*, London: SPG.

Nicholas Usherwood and Paul Holberton, 1987, *The Bible in 20th Century Art*, London: Pagoda Books.

Mark Wallinger, 2001, *Credo*, London: Tate Gallery Publishing.

Hans-Ruedi Weber, 1979, *On a Friday Noon: Meditations Under the Cross*, London: SPCK; Geneva and Grand Rapids: WCC Publications and Wm Eerdmans.

Hans-Ruedi Weber, 1984, *Immanuel: The Coming of Jesus in Art and the Bible*, Geneva, Grand Rapids: WCC Publications and Wm Eerdmans.

Naomi Wray, 1993, *Frank Wesley: Exploring Faith with a Brush (Indian Artist)*, Auckland: Pace Publishing.

Image Packs, Posters, Slide Sets and CD-ROMS

Benedictine Nuns of Turvey Abbey, 2000, *Stations of the Cross* (set of A4 pictures), and 2000, *Jesus, Our Life* (3 series of posters), Great Wakering, Essex: McCrimmons.

Lat Blaylock, *Picturing Jesus: Worldwide Contemporary Artists – Pack A*, 2001, and *Pack B*, 2004, Birmingham: RE Today Services.

Christian Aid posters of Jesus, and packs of pictures for Lent (*The Servant King*) and Advent (*Emmanuel, God With Us*), n.d., www.christian-aid.org.uk.

Church House Publishing, 1999, *Images of Jesus* (traditional and modern), two poster packs, www.chpublishing.co.uk.

Margaret Cooling, 1998, *Jesus Through Art: Resources for Teaching Religious Education and Art*, London: Religious and Moral Education Press.

Margaret Cooling, 2009, *Christianity Through Art*, London: RMEP.

Margaret Cooling, Jane Taylor and Diane Walker, 1998, *Jesus Through Art: A Resource for Teaching Religious Education and Art*, Norwich: SCM-Canterbury Press.

Janet Hodgson, 2006, *The Faith We See: Working with Images of Christ*, Peterborough: Inspire (with CD-ROM).

Janet Hodgson, 2010, *Making the Sign of the Cross: A Creative Resource for Seasonal Worship, Retreats and Quiet Days*, Norwich: Canterbury Press (with CD-ROM).

Images of Salvation: The Story of the Bible through Medieval Art, 2004, CD-ROM, Christianity and Culture, St John's College, Nottingham.

Poster sets – *Jesus Worldwide*, 1991; *Christmas*, 1992; and *Easter*, 1993, Birmingham: RE Today Services.

Slide set – *Christ in Art*, 1987, Birmingham: RE Today Services.

USPG: Anglicans in World Mission, USPG Church of Ireland, CMS, Methodist Church, 2000 (2nd ed.), *The Christ We Share*, and 2002, *Born Among Us*, Resource Packs, London: Methodist Publishing House.

Vie de Jesus Mafa (a set of posters, mini-posters and postcards of 64 illustrations of the gospel from Cameroons), http://www.jesusmafa.com; http://www.biblical-art.com/artist_artwork.asp?id_artist.

Further Reading

Robert Beckford, 1998, *Jesus is Dread: Black Theology and Black Culture in Britain*, London: Darton, Longman and Todd.

John Bell, 2002, *Present on Earth: Worship Resources on the Life of Jesus*, Glasgow: Wild Goose Publications.

Benigno Beltran, 1987, *The Christology of the Inarticulate: An Inquiry into the Filipino Understanding of Jesus*, Manila: Divine Word Publications.

Jose Miguez Bonino, 1977, *Faces of Jesus: Latin American Christologies*, Maryknoll: Orbis Books.

C.W. du Toit (ed.), 1997, *Images of Jesus*, Pretoria: University of South Africa.

Doris Jean Dyke, 1991, *Crucified Woman*, Toronto: United Church Publishing House.

Jim Forest, 2008 (expanded edition), *Praying with Icons*, Maryknoll: Orbis Books.

Norbert Greinacher and Norbert Mette (eds), 1994, *Christianity and Cultures: A Mutual Enrichment*, Concilium 1994, no. 2, London: SCM Press.

Janet Hodgson and Jay Kothare, 1992, *Vision Quest: Native Spirituality and the Church in Canada*, Toronto: Anglican Book Centre Publishing.

Volker Küster, 2001, *The Many Faces of Jesus Christ. Intercultural Christology*, London: SCM Press.

J. N. K. Mugambi and I. Magesa (eds), 1989, *Jesus in African Christianity: Experimentation and Diversity in African Christology*, Nairobi: Initiatives.

Mercy Amba Oduyoye and Musimbi Kanyoro, 1995, *The Will to Arise: Women, Tradition and the Church in Africa*, Maryknoll: Orbis Books.

Jaroslav Pelikan, 1987, *Jesus Through the Centuries: His Place in the History of Culture*, New York: Harper and Row.

G. Schiller (translated by J. Seligman), 1971, *Iconography of Christian Art*, 2 vols, London: Lund Humphries.

Robert Schreiter, 1992, *Faces of Jesus in Africa*, London: SCM Press.

Diane Stinton, 2004, *Jesus of Africa: Voices of Contemporary African Christology*, Maryknoll: Orbis.

R. S. Sugirtharajah (ed.), 1993, *Asian Faces of Jesus*, London: SCM Press.

Anton Wessels, 1986, *Images of Jesus: How Jesus is Perceived and Portrayed in Non-European Cultures*, London: SCM Press.

A Selection of Internet Sources

Churches Advertising Network: http://www.churchads.net; http://www.churchads. net/who/history.html; http://www.churchads.org.uk/live/index.html.

Crosses and Crucifixes: For internet references see Janet Hodgson, 2010, *Making the Sign of the Cross*. Norwich: Canterbury Press.

Early Christian Symbols: http://www.jesuswalk.com/Christian-symbols/ +early+christian+symbols; http://en.wikipedia.org/wiki/Christian_symbolism.

Holding Crosses: www.hadeel.org; www.thechristianshop.co.uk; www.eden.co.uk; www.scotiafairtrade.com; www.holdingcross.com/

William Holman Hunt: http://en.wikipedia.org/wiki//William_Holman_Hunt; http://www.archive.com/archive/H/hunt.html; http://www.squidoo.com/ lightoftheworld-holmanhunt.

Female Christ Figures in Film: www.textweek.com/movies/female_christ.htm; www.informworld.com/index/713800059.pdf.

Images of Jesus and Christ Figure in Film: http://en.wikipedia.org/wiki/ Christ-figure; http://en.wikipedia.org/wiki/Cultural_depictions _of _Jesus; http:// en.wikipedia.org/wiki/Category:Portrayals_of_Jesus_in_film; http://www.unomaha.edu/-jrf/JesusinFilmRein.htm; http://uashome.alaska. edu/-dfgriffin/website/Jesusfilms.htm; http://www.questia.com/library/book/ imaging-the-divine-jesus-and-christ-figures-in-film; http://www.freewebs.com/ thelambandthemouse/ (Christ figures in Disney).

Images of Jesus (some examples): http://members.aol.com/RSISBELL/picture. html; http://spiritlessons.com/Documents/Jesus_Pictures/Jesus_Christ_Pictures. htm (200 pictures); http://picturesofjesus4you.com (300 pictures) and http://

JesusArtUSA.com; http://picturesofjesus4you.com/jesus_cross_/html; http://
openlibrary.org/books/OL11951263M/Jesus_Through_Art; http://en.wikipedia.
org/wiki/Depiction_of_Jesus; www.religionfacts.com/jesus.image_gallery.htm.
Stations of the Cross: http://en.wikipedia.org/wiki/Stations_of_the-Cross; http://
www.stjohncathedral.co.uk/prayers/stations/index.htm.
The Anglican Rosary/Anglican Prayer Beads: http://www.saintgabriels.org/rosary.
html; http://en.wikipedia.org/wiki/Anglican_prayer_beads; http://www.pathguy.
com/rosary.htm; http://www.kingofpeace.org/prayerbeads.htm.
The Rosary: http://www.newadvent.org/cathen/13184b.htm (Catholic
Encyclopedia); http://en.wikipedia.org/wiki/rosary.
Symbols of Jesus: www.fisheaters.com/symbols.html; www.gocek.org/
christiansymbols/; http://en.wikipedia.org/wiki/ichthys; www.symbols.
net/christian/+symbols+of+jesus.

Jesus in Film

King of Kings. Nicholas Ray, 1961, USA.
The Gospel According to St Matthew. Pier Paolo Pasolini, 1964, Italy/France.
The Greatest Story Ever Told. George Stevens, 1965, USA.
The Gospel Road: A Story of Jesus. Robert Elfstrom, 1967, USA.
Godspell. David Greene, 1973, USA.
Jesus Christ Superstar (based on Andrew Lloyd Webber's opera). Norman Jewison,
1973, USA.
The Holy Mountain. Alejandro Jodorowsky, 1973, Mexico/USA.
Monty Python's Life of Brian. Terry Jones, 1979, UK.
Mary and Joseph: A Story of Faith. Eric Till, 1979, Canada.
Jesus of Nazareth. Franco Zeffirelli, 1979, UK/Italy television mini-series.
History of the World, Part 1. Mel Brooks, 1981, USA.
Jesus – The Film (35 episodes). Michael Brynntrup, 1986, Germany.
The Last Temptation of Christ. Martin Scorsese, 1988, USA.
Jesus of Montreal. Denys Arcand, 1989, Canada/France.
Matthew. Reghardt van den Bergh, 1997, USA/South Africa.
Superstar. Bruce McCulloch, 1999, USA.
The Miracle Maker. Animated film, 2000, UK.
The Gospel of John. Philip Saville, 2003, Canada/UK.
The Passion of the Christ. Mel Gibson, 2004, USA.
Color of the Cross. Jean-Claude La Marre, 2006, USA.
Son of Man. Mark Dornford-May, 2006, South Africa.
Anno Domini XXXIII. Melvin Schembri, 2008, Malta.

CD IMAGES AND DISCUSSION QUESTIONS

These images generally connect with the text as indicated. They can of course be used on their own for meditation, reflection and discussion, or as additional imagery for any other chapter.

Preface

(i) *Open Doors and Sundial*, photograph, Robert Cooper.

- Is it time to be open to new ideas and new ways of sharing your faith? (p. xi)

Guidelines for Using the Book

(ii) *The Calling of Peter and Andrew*, early 6th century mosaic, Church of S. Apollinare Nuovo, Ravenna.

- At this time Jesus was often represented as beardless, and his formal stance and gesture reflect the traditional pose of teachers and orators in Graeco-Roman art. Can you recall some of your earliest images of Jesus? What impact did they make on you? (p. 5)

(iii) *African Madonna*, Ukukhanya Kwomhlaba Church, Wembezi, Natal, South Africa.

- How can images of Christ be a resource for holding us closer to God? (p. 7)

Chapter 1: Why Images of Christ?

(iv) Icon of '*Christ, Light of the World*'. Moscow, 16th century.

- What images draw us to Christ in our present day? (p. 13)

(v) *The Barbed Wire Crucifix*, South Africa.

- The original crucifix was fashioned in a workshop with young black people at the height of the liberations struggle in the 1980s, but it is an image that transcend time and space. How does it speak to you? (p. 19)

(vi) *The Light of the World*, Holman Hunt, 19th century, England.

- When in darkness or despair has the light of Christ opened a new door to hope? (p. 21)

(vii) *Lighthouse*, photograph, Robert Cooper.

- What rays of hope can we shine to those overcome by darkness or who are all at sea? (p. 23)

Chapter 2: One Saviour Facing Many Directions

(viii) *Christ meets Zaccheus in Ethiopia*, artist unknown.

- Is Christ calling you to risk coming down and become more involved in the life of your faith community? (p. 27)

(ix) *Heal My Sacred Heart: Christ of the First People*, Mozetti, 1998.

- What ways do we need to forgive from the heart rather than the head? (p. 38)

(x) *Life in its Fullness*, Logo by Bill Powless, Six Nations Reserve, for the former Council on Native Affairs, Anglican Church of Canada.

- How can we draw others into the circle so that all may be one in Christ? (p. 39)

Chapter 3: Working with Images of Christ

(xi) *Mary anoints Jesus' feet*, Alfred Thomas, 1948, *The Life of Christ by an Indian Artist,* London: SPG.

- 'Then took Mary a pound of ointment of spikenard, very costly . . .' What has your faith cost you? (p. 46)

(xii) *Rastafarian Madonna*, Peter, a Guyanese Rasta, 1991, Barbados.

- How do we see Christ in our context today? (p. 55)

Chapter 4: Re-Imaging Mission

(xiii) *Whalton Christ*, 2000.

   - This image is made up of 2850 individual pictures celebrating village life in Whalton, Northumberland. Here the face of Christ is seen in, through and among the people of God and God's creation. Is all our community in our picture of Christ? (p. 67)

(xiv) *Christ in Community*, St George's, Tufnell Park, London, Simon Lord et al.

   - Affixed to the outer wall of the church, this large icon gives visible expression to the Church's vision of mission – that the Christian faith is found and lived in community. What would your visual statement be for your faith community? (p. 71)

(xv) *Christ the Prince of Peace*, Khotso House Tapestry, Johannesburg, South Africa.

   - Christ stands with his suffering people, sharing their struggle for justice and freedom. What can we do about establishing God's justice in our own community and beyond? (p. 76)

Chapter 5: The Young Shall See Visions

(xvi) *Pentecost*, Emma Luyendijk (aged 8 years), South Africa.

   - How can we discover the simple images in us as a way of renewing our faith? (p. 84)

(xvii) *I Am The Way* – a footpath through the cornfield, photograph, Robert Cooper.

   - What path is God calling you to take? (p. 87)

(xviii) *Jesus and the Children*, unknown Chinese artist, 1943, London: SPG, p. 37.

   - What do we hear Jesus saying to us through our children ? (p. 95)

Chapter 6: Praying With Images

(xix) *The Crucifixion*, Coral Bernadine, Barbados, 1980s.

   - The lion and the lamb lie together at the foot of the cross, signifying resolution and hope for the future. Where do you find peace in this image? (p. 108)

(xx) *Be Reconciled to God.*

- The banner of a broken cross hung on the walls of the Anglican cathedral in Pietermaritzburg, South Africa, during the height of the violence in the late 1980s. At the heart of the rupture, where the pain is most intense, the rainbow becomes a symbol of reconciliation. As a pilgrim commented, 'If I want to be close to God then I have to learn to live with open wounds . . . The tapestry helped me understand that when I am faced with pain, I am not alone. The crucified God is with me.' Will your wounds lead to reconciliation and healing? (p. 111)

(xxi) *Field of Sunflowers*, Photograph, Robert Cooper.

- As the sun moves across the sky, sunflowers keep turning to face it. At night they droop their heads. How do we keep turning to the light of Christ to reflect his glory? (p. 117)

Chapter 7: Images That Challenge

(xxii) AIDS icon commissioned by the Chaplaincy to the Arts and Recreation group, Durham Diocese. Design and calligraphy by Ewan Clayton. Woodwork by Peter Jones. Photograph by Robert Cooper.

- The words read 'Christ has AIDS'. How do you feel using such imagery with Christ today? (p. 124)

(xxiii) *Jesa Christa Crucified*, unknown South African artist, Paternoster, South Africa.

- How can such figures embrace all who are being crucified today? (p. 133)

(xxiv) *The Power and the Glory*, 1985, Coral Bernadine, Barbados.

- What images can strengthen our faith? (p. 135)